LIFE-CHANGING
BIBLE
VERSES
YOU SHOULD
KNOW

ERWIN & REBECCA
LUTZER

HARVEST HOUSE PUBLISHERS

EUGENE, OREGON

Cover by Dugan Design Group, Bloomington, Minnesota

Cover photo by Kristy-Anne Glubish / Design Pics Inc. / Alamy

Back cover photo of authors by Jim and Mary Whitmer, Wheaton, Illinois

LIFE-CHANGING BIBLE VERSES YOU SHOULD KNOW
Copyright © 2011 by Erwin and Rebecca Lutzer
Published by Harvest House Publishers
Eugene, Oregon 97402
www.harvesthousepublishers.com

Library of Congress Cataloging-in-Publication Data
Lutzer, Erwin W.
    Life-changing Bible verses you should know / Erwin and Rebecca Lutzer.
        p. cm.
    ISBN 978-0-7369-3952-2 (pbk.)
    ISBN 978-0-7369-4123-5 (eBook)
    1. Bible—Memorizing. 2. Bible—Quotations. I. Lutzer, Rebecca. II. Title.
    BS617.7.L88 2011
    242'.5—dc22
                                                                    2011012493

This book is dedicated to our
delightful grandchildren

Jack, Samuel, Emma, Anna, Abigail, Owen, Evelyn

with our earnest prayer that from childhood they will
know the Holy Scriptures which are able to make
them wise for salvation through faith in Jesus Christ.

2 Timothy 3:15

CONTENTS

Part 2: Additional Bible Memory Verses for the Topics in this Book

FROM OUR HEARTS TO YOURS

The purpose of this book is to bring about real change in your life—the kind that happens when you take the time to both memorize Scripture passages and grow in your understanding of the basic doctrines and teachings of the Bible. When we as Christians want to nurture a stronger faith and grow in "the grace and knowledge of our Lord and Savior Jesus Christ" (2 Peter 3:18), it is necessary for us to store up God's Word within our souls and minds. This discipline lies at the heart of Christian maturity.

Whether you have been a Christian for many years or you have just recently come to know about the Christian faith, this book is for you. In fact, we pray that it will be of great benefit to anyone who is serious about having their lives changed by unleashing the power of God's Word. Tragically, the practice of memorizing Scripture is rarely emphasized today in families and churches. For when we make an effort to hide God's Word in our hearts, it will...

- help keep us from sin
- encourage us to be faithful
- sustain us in times of great need
- comfort us in times of sorrow and pain
- direct us in times of uncertainty, and
- strengthen us in times of weakness

We have often wished there was a resource that offers a comprehensive selection of Scripture verses that focus on the critical aspects of our faith and doctrine—one that we can use as an aid to memorizing key Bible verses. Although we should study all the Scriptures, there are certain verses that are especially worthy of our attention because they speak directly to the most important issues of life, giving encouragement and strength in time of need. The verses in this book were selected by answering two simple questions:

- What topics would be most appropriate for critical aspects of Christian living?
- What are the summary verses that encapsulate the heart of these scriptural teachings?

The structure of this book is easy to follow. The verses are listed at the beginning of each chapter and are followed by a commentary explaining the meaning and significance of these passages. At the end of each chapter you'll find questions that are useful for either individual discipleship or group study. Our hope is that you will both memorize these life-changing passages and come to understand their important place in our lives.

There are nearly 40 chapters that introduce us to a bit over 100 life-changing Bible verses. If you choose to study one chapter a week and use this book over a period of 40 weeks (or you go at whatever pace works best for you), you'll develop a strong grasp on the truths that reside at the heart of the Christian faith. And if you take the time to memorize these passages, you will see real—and lasting—change in your life. That is what the Bible itself repeatedly promises.

Together let us prove this promise of Scripture: "The word of God is alive and active. Sharper than any double-edged sword, it penetrates even to dividing soul and spirit, joints and marrow; it judges the thoughts and attitudes of the heart" (Hebrews 4:12). Joshua was promised that he would be successful if he meditated on the law of God "day and night" (Joshua 1:8). This is another promise we can claim for ourselves.

An American couple bought a jewelry box in France that they were told would glow in the dark. When they brought it home, they discovered, to their chagrin, it did not glow during the night. Essentially it was no different than the other boxes on their dresser. When they gave it to a friend who knew French, he read the instructions, which said, "Put me in the sunshine during the day and I will glow in the dark." Sure enough, when the box was exposed to sunshine during the day, it emitted radiance during the night.

Memorizing Scripture and retaining it within us is like that jewelry box retaining sunshine during the day in preparation for the coming night. When we go through trials, we often wonder how we can make it through another day or another week. Or when a temptation wreaks havoc with our lives, we find ourselves feeling overwhelmed or discouraged. Only God's Word—stored up in our hearts and minds—can rebuke us, cleanse us, keep us from sin, and enable us to cope with life's challenges.

We are dedicating this book to our grandchildren, even though at the time of this writing they are yet too young to understand the commentary for themselves. Even so, some of them are already memorizing Scripture, and we are praying that as they grow older, they will maintain a lifetime of Scripture memorization and grow to love the truths at the heart of the Christian faith.

Join us on a journey of getting to know these Bible verses that have the power to change your life!

Part 1:

KEY BIBLE
VERSES YOU
SHOULD KNOW

ADVERSITY

Psalm 46:1—*God is our refuge and strength, an ever-present help in trouble.*

1 Peter 1:6-7—*In all this you greatly rejoice, though now for a little while you may have had to suffer grief in all kinds of trials. These have come so that the proven genuineness of your faith—of greater worth than gold, which perishes even though refined by fire—may result in praise, glory and honor when Jesus Christ is revealed.*

When we think back to the devastating earthquake in Haiti that killed nearly 200,000 people, many images come to mind, but one image that stands out well above the others is that of a young mother being interviewed on television as she held a baby in her arms.

"I lost my son…he died in the rubble."

"Did you get to bury him?"

"No, no chance; his body was crushed in the rubble; I just had to throw him away."

Just then the camera zeroed in on her backpack as she prepared to board a bus. Stuffed in a side pocket was a Bible. As she boarded the bus she could be heard, speaking to no one in particular, saying, "God is our refuge and strength, an ever-present help in trouble…" Her voice trailed off as she disappeared from view.

When the report was over we just kept staring at the television for a while, pushing back tears and letting what we'd just seen sink into our souls. A dead child with no chance to plan a funeral and pay respects to her precious little one, a baby in her arms, and she was boarding a bus that was going she knew not where. Yet she still expressed belief; she still trusted that God is her refuge and strength.

Faith in adversity!

This mother—God bless her—began quoting Psalm 46, which was written as a praise song after God spared the city of Jerusalem from an invasion by Assyrians who were threatening to annihilate the inhabitants. In the midst of a harrowing escape, the Israelites found God to be an unshakable pillar.

God is our refuge. A refuge is a safe place you can run to for shelter when life's storms are swirling around you. No wonder this dear mother found solace in this psalm, which continues, "Therefore we will not fear, though the earth give way and the mountains fall into the heart of the sea, though its waters roar and foam and the mountains quake with their surging" (verses 2-3).

Yes, the mountains did give way and fall into the heart of the sea, but God is unaffected by the fluctuation on events of earth; He is always there, solid, unmoved. When the mountains are shaking and the ground beneath you is quaking, run to God, and He will meet you. Yes, even when our world falls apart in the aftermath of a horrendous natural disaster, God is unchanging and remains with us.

In the midst of the devastation, God is our source of supply. The psalm continues, "There is a river whose streams make glad the city of God, the holy place where the Most High dwells" (verse 4). Most likely that refers to a tunnel that had been built some time earlier to bring water into the city in case it was ever besieged. The people of Jerusalem saw this provision as God giving them specific help at their time of their need.

Then the psalm gives us a command: "Be still, and know that I am God; I will be exalted among the nations, I will be exalted in the earth" (verse 10). Let us cease striving and let God be God. Even in adversity He is there; or perhaps we should say *especially in adversity* He is there!

Adversity should not drive us away from God; rather, it should drive us into His arms. He is there for the grieving mother, and for the family that has experienced indescribable loss. The psalm ends, "The LORD Almighty is with us; the God of Jacob is our fortress" (verse 11).

God wants to be believed. And our faith is more precious to Him than gold, which perishes. When we continue to trust Him even when there appears to be no reason to do so—and we go on believing God's bare Word, our faith will "result in praise, glory and honor when Jesus Christ is revealed" (1 Peter 1:7).

Reverend Henry F. Lyte was a pastor in Scotland who battled tuberculosis most of his life. On his final Sunday, September 4, 1847, amid many tears the congregation sang a song he himself had composed, "Abide with Me." It spoke of the unchanging God in an ever-changing world:

> Abide with me; fast falls the eventide;
> The darkness deepens; Lord, with me abide.
> When other helpers fail and comforts flee,
> Help of the helpless, O abide with me.
>
> Swift to its close ebbs out life's little day;
> Earth's joys grow dim; its glories pass away;
> Change and decay in all around I see;
> O Thou who changest not, abide with me.
>
> Hold Thou Thy cross before my closing eyes;
> Shine through the gloom and point me to the skies.
> Heav'n's morning breaks, and earth's vain shadows flee;
> In life, in death, O Lord, abide with me.

The young mother in Haiti—who was clutching an undernourished baby in her arms and had no time to mourn the tragic death of her son—found solace in the God who was still beside her when the earth gave way. "God is our refuge and strength," she said amid her grief and uncertainty of the future.

In times of adversity, our faith can hold fast. And God is both honored and pleased.

Taking God's Word to Heart

1. Reflect on the account of the Haitian mother who tragically lost her son. How has Psalm 46 been a source of strength for you during adversity? What other Scripture passages do you turn to for help in difficult times?

2. What does it mean to you that God is your refuge? In life's journey, why is God's unchangeable nature a source of strength for us?

3. Recall an instance when God provided timely help for a specific need. What did that experience teach or confirm for you about God's character?

4. What are some ways God has used adversity to shape your life?

5. Why is God honored and pleased when we exercise faith in times of adversity?

ANXIETY

Matthew 6:33-34—*Seek first his kingdom and his righteousness, and all these things will be given to you as well. Therefore do not worry about tomorrow, for tomorrow will worry about itself. Each day has enough trouble of its own.*

Someone has said that people live their lives "crucified between two thieves—the regrets of yesterday and the anxieties of tomorrow."

The word *worry* means "to be torn in two." And that is exactly what anxiety does—it tears us apart. Our bodies might obediently go in one direction, but our minds are somewhere else. The result is that we live with tension; we cannot sleep at night and we cannot enjoy ourselves during the day. Worry causes us to work against ourselves and hinders our fellowship with God.

Don't you wish that you could worry, say, from 8:00 p.m. to about 8:30 p.m., then turn off that anxiety to get a good night's rest? But we can't seem to prevent worry from returning to our minds. Worry is like an out-of-control blip on a TV screen that flits wherever it wishes without asking permission or responding to our wishes. We are the victims of worry, and we can't prevent it from intruding uninvited into our minds.

When speaking to His disciples, Jesus gave us three reasons we should not worry, and then three reasons we don't have to worry. First, He said we should not worry because of who we are. "Look at the birds of the air; they do not sow or reap or store away in barns, and yet your heavenly Father feeds them. Are you not much more valuable than they?" (Matthew 6:26). If God takes care of the birds, will He not take care of us? Don't miss Jesus' point: When we worry, we diminish our value!

Second, we should not worry because it is useless. "Can any one of you by worrying add a single hour to your life?" (verse 27). Worry is like putting on the brakes and stepping on the gas simultaneously. It would be worth it if worry added to the length of our life; but in fact, it might diminish it. Worry changes nothing.

Third, we should not worry because of our testimony. "For the pagans run after all these things, and your heavenly Father knows that you need them" (verse 32). When we worry, we act like the pagans who do not know the heavenly Father. Suppose two people are told they have cancer—one is a Christian, and the other is not. How tragic it would be if the Christian accepted such news in the same way as the pagan!

But how do we overcome worry or anxiety? Three words in this narrative will help us. First, there is the word *Father*. We find it more difficult to trust our heavenly Father than our earthly father because our heavenly Father is less predictable. Our earthly father would prevent us from having cancer and accidents if it were within his power to do so. But our heavenly Father does not. Does that mean that He loves us less?

No, our heavenly Father loves us with a perfect love. But He is willing to allow us to experience loss and pain for a greater, eternal good. Please believe us when we say that your heavenly Father is trustworthy. He loves you and will do right by you!

The second word is *faith*. "O you of little faith," Jesus said. Our faith must be developed; we must believe that God is not only powerful, but good. Faith is built through an understanding of God's promises.

And the third word is *first*. "Seek first his kingdom and his righteousness, and all these things will be given to you as well" (verse 33). Worry reminds us of all those things that we have not yet given to God. Or, we could say that our worries point to those things that we have placed ahead of God.

By entrusting ourselves to our heavenly Father, we no longer have to be torn in two by the events of life. They have been transferred from our hands to His, and with that we can be content.

How does this apply if you are dealing with a crisis such as a fatal disease? We must be convinced of two facts: (1) that all matters are in God's hands, and (2) that God is good and trustworthy.

As Christians we must transfer our anxieties from our shoulders to God's. This transfer must be made consciously and daily. "Cast all your anxiety on him because he cares for you" (1 Peter 5:7). This does not mean we will never have another worry; it does not mean we will be free from emotional pain. But it does mean we can have confidence that God is there for us, today and tomorrow. It means we can live with hope.

Suppose you were on an airliner and asked the flight attendant to check on the pilots to make sure they have not fallen asleep as the plane begins its trek across the ocean. The attendant would likely be exasperated with you, and properly say, "You are insulting our pilots!" And, yes, you *would* be insulting the pilots. How much better it would be for you to simply relax and say, "I have committed myself to this airplane and have reason to believe that although I've never met the pilots, I have confidence they can be trusted."

When we constantly bombard God with pleas to do this and that—to take care of one thing or another—we often also insult Him. What we need is not more words sent in His direction, but a genuine transfer of our anxieties to Him. We are with Him on the plane, so to speak, and we have to trust that He, as our pilot, will take us wherever He wills. He will take us across oceans and land us safely on the other side.

There is a story about a woman who was waiting for a bus and carrying a heavy suitcase. She was so glad when she saw the bus come; she paid the fare and then stood in the aisle holding up the suitcase. Someone said to her, "Why don't you put the suitcase on the floor?" to which she replied, "I am so thankful that the bus is carrying me. I can't expect it to carry my suitcase too!"

If you are a Christian, you are on the bus. God is taking us en route to His heavenly kingdom. There is simply no reason for you to carry the weight that is already in God's hands. You must put down the suitcase. Since the governments of the world will one day be upon Christ's shoulders, He most assuredly can bear up when our anxiety is added to His other responsibilities!

And if the anxiety returns? We are to reject those thoughts and keep reaffirming that we are in God's hands.

We know that God's eyes are on the sparrow, and most assuredly they are on us too!

Taking God's Word to Heart

1. Describe what it means to worry. Unchecked, what can worry do to us?

2. Read Matthew 6:25-34. Discuss the three reasons Jesus gave us for not engaging in worry. What was His logic behind each?

3. What steps do you take to overcome worry? What three words in Matthew 6:30-34 describe the key to overcoming worry?

4. How strong is your faith? As believers, in what ways do we develop our faith?

5. How can we effectively act on the truth of 1 Peter 5:7? Describe what it means to place our care in God's hands.

THE ARMOR OF GOD

Ephesians 6:10-11—*Be strong in the Lord and in his mighty power. Put on the full armor of God, so that you can take your stand against the devil's schemes.*

We've all heard the saying that God loves you and has a wonderful plan for your life. But the corollary is that Satan hates you and has a destructive plan for your life. There is a devil in this world, and he is God's adversary. He was created by God but fell into the sin of pride and established his own dark, evil kingdom, and he wants us to be a part of it. It's even possible that he has already made plans for our individual downfall. Though he can be in only one place at a time, he gives the illusion of being omnipresent because he has demons who do his bidding. Satan's name means "adversary," and another of his names, the devil, means "accuser" or "slanderer."

Satan injects thoughts into our minds that he wants us to believe are our own. A good example is what happened to Ananias and Sapphira, who lied when they said they had given the church all the money they received from the sale of their land, when in reality they kept back a part of the price (Acts 5:1-10). Note that Peter asked Ananias, "How is it that Satan has so filled your heart that you have lied to the Holy Spirit…?" (verse 3). Think about it: If the couple had realized that it was the devil who put those deceitful plans into their minds, they would have been terrified. But because the devil can't be seen and because they believed this deceptive idea was their own, they were not afraid to tell a lie.

When we open our minds and hearts to sin, Satan will inject wrong thoughts into our minds. This is usually the source of divisiveness, hatred, false guilt, anger, immorality, rebellion, and our tolerance of occult practices. Often a so-called demonic problem is actually a sin problem. As a friend of ours says, "When you get rid of the garbage, the flies leave!"

No wonder Paul says, "Put on the full armor of God, so that you can take your stand against the devil's schemes" (Ephesians 6:11). If you are a Christian and you think you aren't in a battle or that Satan isn't interested in you, maybe it's because you are not a threat to him. Or, perhaps you are self-deceived.

Please read Ephesians 6:10-18, where Paul lists the pieces of the "armor of God" that will protect us from Satan's deceptions. Paul imagines us in a wrestling match with the devil and his forces, and it is a fight to the finish.

The first piece of armor Paul lists is the belt of truth. In those days, a soldier's belt held everything together. When he wasn't in direct combat, much of his equipment hung from his belt. The "belt of truth" is of course a reference to the truth that is established by God and revealed through His Word (John 17:17). Wearing this belt keeps us from believing error and entertaining known or unknown deceptions.

John Bunyan, in his book *The Holy War,* described the battle for the mind that we are all involved in. In the book, Diabolus and other demons discuss how they were going to trick and deceive people. Remember, their goal is to find an opening into "man's soul." One of the demons talked strategy: "We will cajole and tempt them, but in the end we will lie, lie, lie." That is Satan's scheme, and the belt of truth exposes these lies.

Satan hates truth and speaks truth only when he must. In the New Testament, when demons were in the presence of Jesus, they said, "[We] know who you are—the Holy One of God!" (Mark 1:24). They spoke the truth, but only because they *had* to.

The other pieces of armor follow: the breastplate of righteousness, the shoes of the gospel of peace, the shield of faith, the helmet of salvation, and the sword of the Spirit.

How do we put on these various pieces of armor?

First, we put them on by prayer. Paul said, "Pray in the Spirit on all occasions with all kinds of prayers" (verse 18). To pray "in the Spirit" means much more than saying the right words; it is prayer that comes from a yielded heart and that grows out of the promises of God's Word. It means that we begin each day not merely committing our day to God, but affirming our desire to be shielded from the temptations that surely will come.

Second, we should not think these pieces of armor can be put on individually, as if we can go into battle with some of the pieces but not others. Looked at in one way, we must put on all the pieces of armor if we want to stand against "the spiritual forces of evil in the heavenly realms" (verse 12). Therefore, we must see the armor of God as a lifestyle; it must become a part of who we are as believers. Our lives must be characterized by truth, righteousness, a readiness to share the gospel. We must live a life of faith, be secure in our salvation, and know how to both study and use God's Word. Satan does not flee because we use the right words, important though that might be. Rather, he flees when he sees a believer marked by the integrity of a single-minded devotion to God and His Word.

At The Moody Church, where we attend and serve, there is a roof deck designed to accommodate up to 250 people. Because it is outside, we have had a persistent problem with pigeons descending and resting on the deck, which, as you can imagine, causes cleanup problems. Our trustees had a brilliant idea: They purchased a tape that recorded the sounds of a falcon killing a pigeon. This tape plays approximately every two minutes on the roof deck. As you might guess, ever since we installed the tape, there has never been a pigeon in sight!

Satan likes to taunt us, claiming great power and frightening us with threats of our eventual destruction. But, like a tape playing on a roof deck, these threats are empty if we are dressed with the armor of God. Satan might intimidate us, but he has already been soundly defeated by Christ. His screech of so-called victory over us is actually a howl of defeat.

We can stand in the evil day, for He who is for us is greater than he who is against us (1 John 4:4). But let's not neglect our armor!

Taking God's Word to Heart

1. With the story of Ananias and Sapphira in mind, think of the kinds of temptations that come to us via our minds and how Satan might be involved in them.

2. How many Bible passages can you think of that speak of Satan's activities in relationship to our temptations? And what do we learn from these passages about how to resist the devil? (See especially James 4:6-10; 1 Peter 5:6-10.)

3. "Often a so-called demonic problem is actually a sin problem." List sins that we tolerate that might give the devil an opportunity to influence us (for an example, see Ephesians 4:26-27).

4. With your Bible open to Ephesians 6:10-20, list the pieces of the armor we are to put on. Next to each one, write a description of what you think it should mean with regard to our lives.

5. Using Jesus as our example, how can we use Scripture in response to Satan's assaults?

ASSURANCE

*Romans 8:15-16—The Spirit you received does not
make you slaves, so that you live in fear again; rather,
the Spirit you received brought about your adoption to
sonship. And by him we cry, "Abba, Father." The Spirit
himself testifies with our spirit that we are God's children.*

*1 John 5:13—I write these things to you who
believe in the name of the Son of God so that
you may know that you have eternal life.*

One of God's most blessed gifts to us is the assurance of our salvation. As a boy I prayed often, asking Jesus to "come into my heart." But because I didn't feel any different afterward, I assumed I wasn't "born again." When I was about 14 my parents counseled, "You have to receive Christ by faith," and so I knelt down once again and said, "By faith I receive Christ now as Savior." After that I had an overwhelming sense of peace and confidence; I strongly sensed God's presence and was confident that I knew Him. And that sense of confidence—that settled assurance—has never left me.

People from other religions don't have such personal assurance. For example, many Muslims are convinced that Islam is the right religion, but they have no confidence that when they die, they will arrive in heaven. I've heard Muslims say, "I do my best and I hope I'm going to heaven, but I have no idea what Allah is going to do." The same can be said for people of other religions. Only Christ can grant personal assurance because He alone has the qualifications to be a Savior.

What is the basis of our assurance? First, it is based on Jesus' death and resurrection on our behalf. If you believe that when Jesus died and arose again He did all that ever will be necessary for you to be saved—if you embrace this for yourself—you will be saved and know it. For in response to such faith we are given the gift of the Holy Spirit, who confirms that we are God's children. We have an overwhelming sense of confidence that we belong to God because we trust His promises.

There are several reasons some people lack assurance of their salvation. One is that there is a branch of Christendom that wrongly teaches that salvation is a cooperative effort between us and God. If you do your part, God will do His part. Understandably, you can have no assurance if you think that salvation is partially dependent on your good works, for there is no way of knowing whether your works are good enough. And the Bible teaches they never are! (see Ephesians 2:8-9 and Titus 3:5).

Those who believe their sin is greater than God's grace also lack assurance. Some time ago I (Erwin) spoke with a woman who taught a Bible study and had even led people to Christ, but doubted her own salvation. I told her the story of a man who had to cross a frozen lake, and, fearing that the ice would not hold him, got down on his hands and knees to evenly distribute his weight on the ice as he crawled along. Then he looked up and saw a team of horses approaching from behind him. He realized that if the ice could hold the horses, it most assuredly could hold him! So immediately he got up and walked with confidence.

I said to this woman, "The ice beneath all who have trusted Jesus is equally thick. Some of us are walking along and enjoying it, but you are walking on all fours in fear; it is time for you to stand up with renewed faith in Christ!" Jesus is capable of saving every sinner who believes on Him.

Yet another reason people lack assurance of their salvation is that they might not have received Christ as their Savior in the first place! They have never really believed in Jesus as their Lord and Savior. They may have prayed a prayer but still not know salvation because prayer does not save us; only a personal transfer of trust to Jesus can give them His forgiveness and acceptance. They might not sense personal assurance because they have developed their own sense of self-confidence as a result of believing that salvation is just a matter of being good.

What a difference personal assurance makes! Usually when we go to an airport we'll have confirmed tickets in hand, but occasionally we've flown standby. When we do, we wait anxiously, not knowing whether we will hear our names called so we can board the airplane. But when we have tickets in our hands, we are able to relax because we know seats have been reserved for us on the flight.

When James Simpson, the first person to use chloroform in surgery, was dying, he was asked, "What is your speculation regarding your future?" He answered, "I have no speculation," and then he quoted 2 Timothy 1:12: "I know whom I have believed, and am convinced that he is able to guard what I have entrusted to him until that day."

Through faith in Christ today, you can have a confirmed ticket. "I write these things to you who believe in the name of the Son of God so that you may know that you have eternal life" (1 John 5:13). Admit your sinfulness and accept what Jesus did for you on the cross and in His resurrection—and a place will be reserved for you in heaven.

Taking God's Word to Heart

1. Describe your understanding of the concept of "personal assurance."

2. Why is Jesus' death and resurrection the basis of our assurance? Why is our response of faith in His death and resurrection so important?

3. Some who lack assurance believe their sin is greater than God's grace. How would you respond to that?

4. How does believing in Jesus for eternal life provide answers for the reasons that a person might lack assurance?

5. Second Timothy 1:12 provides one of the great affirmations of Scripture. How do you understand the relationship of faith to assurance?

CHARACTER

Psalm 15:1-2—*L*ORD, *who may dwell in your sacred tent? Who may live on your holy mountain? The one whose walk is blameless, who does what is righteous, who speaks the truth from their heart.*

Philippians 2:14-15—*Do everything without grumbling or arguing, so that you may become blameless and pure, "children of God without fault in a warped and crooked generation." Then you will shine among them like stars in the sky.*

D.L. Moody said quite accurately that character is what a man is in the dark. Unfortunately, our generation finds it difficult to distinguish character from reputation. In our careless generation, only one's reputation seems to matter. But our character is more important than our reputation. People can damage your reputation, but they cannot damage your character.

Yale law professor Stephen Carter defines character (he calls it integrity) as something very specific, and it requires three steps, (a) *discerning* what is right and wrong; (b) *acting* on what you have discerned, even at personal cost; and (c) *saying openly* that you are acting on your understanding of right from wrong.[1] In other words, a person of character should not be ashamed that he or she is living with deeply held convictions. The more public we are about our commitment to integrity, the more motivated we will be to live by our standards.

Psalm 15 asks and answers these questions: "LORD, who may dwell in your sacred tent? Who may live on your holy mountain?" (verse 1). Then what follows is a description of the man whom God receives, the one who is allowed to scale the hill of the Lord and be pleasing to Him. We can do no better than to walk though this psalm to identify and contemplate the lifestyle of the person who has the kind of character that pleases God.

First, such a person speaks the truth: "The one whose walk is blameless, who does what is righteous, who speaks the truth from their heart; whose tongue utters no slander" (verses 2-3). He speaks the truth no matter what—even when it diminishes him, or it requires putting other people in better light, or it means making a painful confession.

A person of character speaks the truth even when it shames him. Recently we heard about a Christian leader who, when confronted with the accusation of having an affair on the Internet, denied it—until the evidence was presented to him. Our penchant to hide sin is so powerful that it is almost impossible to speak the truth about ourselves *to* ourselves, much less to others!

The person of character speaks the truth even when it indicts him. We heard about a man who claimed injuries on the job when, in reality, he was injured in a hunting accident. He will receive workmen's compensation for the rest of his life. When a visiting minister told this man that he should confess to the compensation board, he responded, "Do you think I want to go to jail?" This man not only lost his integrity, but when confronted, neither did he want to pay the price of getting it back.

The person of integrity also honors friendships; he is the one "whose tongue utters no slander, who does no wrong to a neighbor, and casts no slur on others" (verse 3). Someone has said, "If you want to find out who your friends are, just make one big, public mistake." To a man of character, his friend's reputation will be as important as his own.

He also keeps commitments. He "who despises a vile person but honors those who fear the Lord; who keeps an oath even when it hurts" (verse 4). *He keeps his oath even when it hurts!* He keeps his word even when he regrets the promise he has made.

Finally, he refuses to take advantage of others. He "lends money to the poor without interest; who does not accept a bribe against the innocent" (verse 5). We should not interpret this to mean that he might accept a bribe against someone who is not innocent. No, the text simply means that he is the kind of person who cannot be bought. He will not up his prices just because he thinks he can get away with it. He doesn't take advantage of others.

In the New Testament, the apostle Paul connects character and our witness for Christ. We are to be "blameless and pure, 'children of God without fault,'" and in so doing, our character will shine like a star in a dark night (Philippians 2:15). In fact, without character, our witness is muted or even destroyed.

Character is fragile. It is like a vase on a mantel shelf that, after it falls to the floor, shatters, and is glued back together again, still evidences some hairline cracks showing where it was damaged. When a youth pastor asked me (Erwin) for some ministry advice, I said, "Guard your integrity...guard your character; it is your most precious possession. If you lose it, it might be impossible for you to get it back."

Character is the foundation of all other virtues.

Taking God's Word to Heart

1. How do you define character? Why is character important to you? Explain how Psalm 15:1-2 defines character.

2. Discuss the characteristics of a person with integrity. What happens to our integrity when we fail to align our thoughts, words, and actions with the truth?

3. Why is personal character important to our witness for Christ?

4. Do you strive to always keep your commitments? Keeping a commitment may come at a personal cost. Are you willing to preserve your integrity in this arena, whatever it costs?

Recall an instance when someone broke a commitment that was costly to you.

5. In the course of life and its ever-challenging circumstances, one's character is a fragile possession. What steps do you take to guard your character?

CONSCIENCE

Hebrews 10:22—*Let us draw near to God with a
sincere heart and with the full assurance that faith brings,
having our hearts sprinkled to cleanse us from a guilty
conscience and having our bodies washed with pure water.*

1 John 3:21-22—*Dear friends, if our hearts do
not condemn us, we have confidence before God
and receive from him anything we ask, because we
keep his commands and do what pleases him.*

A clear conscience is a powerful motivation to serve the Lord with joy and peace.

The conscience is that faculty of our souls that sits in judgment of all we do, either approving or disapproving of our actions. As someone said, it is that part of us that makes us feel as if we are being watched. Although we have grown up in different cultures with different parents and different expectations, we have all felt the condemning voice of our conscience, which tells us when we have "messed up." And, like a ketchup stain on a white shirt, a blot on our soul will not disappear without a strong detergent. Just ask Lady Macbeth, a Shakespeare character who thought that if she washed her bloody hands in water the guilt of murder would be easily washed away. But she discovered that the water didn't make her hands clean; rather, her hands made the river bloody!

The New Testament speaks of four different kinds of consciences. First, there is a *weak* conscience (1 Corinthians 8:7). This refers to Christians in the apostle Paul's day who thought it was a sin to eat meat that had been sacrificed to idols. They were not aware that, as believers, they could now eat such meat because their loyalty to Jesus canceled their loyalty to the pagan gods they formerly worshiped. This reminds us that although some things are always wrong and some things are always right, there are also some things that are a matter of personal conscience to be determined by each person.

Second, there is a *dead* conscience. This is the conscience within a person who is so determined to sin or maintain his hypocrisy that his inner voice is silenced. "Such teachings come through hypocritical liars, whose consciences have been seared as with a hot iron" (1 Timothy 4:2). Such a person could, over time, become a sociopath who hurts others without feeling the slightest twinge of guilt or regret.

Third, there is the *defiled* conscience. "To the pure, all things are pure, but to those who are corrupted and do not believe, nothing is pure. In fact, both their minds and consciences are corrupted" (Titus 1:15). Think of the immoral man who keeps his sin carefully hidden but must live with himself day after day. He can enjoy nothing pure because everything he does and thinks is corrupted.

Finally, there is the *good* conscience, the conscience that can empower us to do what is right, and give us courage and strength whether we are experiencing success or failure. A good conscience is one that is free from accusations. Again, we turn to Paul: "I strive always to keep my conscience clear before God and man" (Acts 24:16). Of course at one time Paul's conscience was not clear at all—remember that before his conversion to Christianity, he was jailing believers and even agreed to have them killed.

So the question for you and us is this: How can we have a good or clear conscience? There are two parts to the answer. The first is to confess our sins and receive God's cleansing for our conscience. "If we confess our sins, he is faithful and just and will forgive us our sins and purify us from all unrighteousness" (1 John 1:9). To confess our sins means that we agree with God about our sin—we honestly admit what we have done, taking full responsibility for all our actions. When we do this, we not only receive God's forgiveness, but we are cleansed "from all unrighteousness." That means that the self-hatred and condemnation that comes after we do wrong is wiped away. If we believe that what God says is true, we no longer need be plagued by guilt and needless regret.

The second aspect to clearing our conscience has to do with our relationships with other people. Remember, Paul said he had a clear conscience "before God and man." Often when we sin, there has to be reconciliation between us and others. The person who has committed adultery must come clean about their sin by talking with a counselor, and almost certainly by confessing to his or her spouse. The person who has cheated his or her company has to confess it and accept the consequences. The person who has erupted in anger against a spouse, a child, or a friend must ask for forgiveness.

Whatever stands in the way of fellowship with others has to be confronted so we can enjoy a clear conscience. The famous golfer Tiger Woods actually expressed relief when his many affairs were exposed. His guilty conscience was a distraction that gave him no peace. Painful though it was to confess in the midst of his embarrassment and shame, he no longer had to make the constant effort to hide his dalliances.

The rewards of a clear conscience are huge, "Dear friends, if our hearts do not condemn us, we have confidence before God and receive from him anything we ask, because we keep his commands and do what pleases him" (1 John 3:21-22). We can both work and sleep with peace in our hearts because our conscience approves of all we do.

With our conscience at rest, we have the confidence that we can witness to our faith with confidence and joy.

Taking God's Word to Heart

1. What does one's conscience do?
2. A clear conscience can be a powerful incentive. What are some by-products of a clear conscience?

3. Discuss the four kinds of conscience described in the New Testament. What typifies each?

4. What can we do to maintain a clear conscience?

5. Focus on 1 John 3:21-22. What does this passage tell us about the rewards of a clear conscience?

COURAGE

Joshua 1:7-8—*Be strong and very courageous. Be careful to obey all the law my servant Moses gave you; do not turn from it to the right or to the left, that you may be successful wherever you go. Keep this Book of the Law always on your lips; meditate on it day and night, so that you may be careful to do everything written in it. Then you will be prosperous and successful.*

When God gave Joshua the command to be "very courageous," Joshua was about to lead his troops into a huge battle. You can imagine the fear and apprehension of any military commander on the eve of conflict, when he is only too aware that some of his men might be killed, and conceivably, the war might go against him. In other words, he could lose. Moses was dead, and the young Joshua had to face the reality of the formidable city of Jericho on his own. This command to be courageous was accompanied with this promise: "The LORD your God will be with you wherever you go" (Joshua 1:9). In other words, courage was not to be found within himself but by looking beyond himself, depending on the help of his own invisible Commander.

We as believers never have to face the harsh realities of life on our own. Here is God's personal promise to us: "Never will I leave you; never will I forsake you" (Hebrews 13:5). God walks with us on good days and bad, on days when we are promoted and days when we are demoted. When we are bereaved, or we face a terminal illness, God is there with us.

Truth be told, it is one thing to know these promises and quite another to be comforted by them. There are a couple reasons we are tempted to lack courage even though the Lord is with us. One is because we know that the promise of God's presence does not guarantee we will be free of trouble. Christians through the ages have faced poverty, loneliness, the loss of loved ones, and every crisis imaginable. Just recently we were told of a young mother dying of cancer and leaving her three children behind. Yes, God is with her, but His presence has not brought healing or deliverance. Her children are confused because they fear the future.

Another reason we're tempted to lack courage is that the assurance of God's presence does not do away with our personal struggles with sin, broken relationships, and regrets. These disappointments befall us all. We should be encouraged to remember that even Jesus, whose trust in the Father never wavered, cringed during His prayer in Gethsemane as He anticipated the horror that awaited Him.

How, then, do we apply these promises despite the fact we have no assurance we will be delivered from what we fear? The answer is twofold: First, we know that God can take even the bad things in our lives and work them out for our good. We are convinced that He has a purpose in our trials that lies beyond the human eye. Yes, He has higher purposes that we can only dimly see in this life. So when we are not delivered from that which gives us fear, we need to remember God is allowing it for our good and His glory.

Second, we are assured that even our doubts and sorrows do not separate us from God's love and care. In moments when we are weak, God is still with us, walking through our wilderness, directing, providing for, and comforting us. Even when we lack faith, God is faithful. We must remember we live by promises, not explanations.

The night Joshua was to attack Jericho, he was given a vision, a divine apparition while on a stroll around Jericho, thinking and planning how he would defeat the city. A man appeared in the darkness (we have reason to believe this was a pre-incarnate visitation of Christ).

Joshua was terrified, and so, thinking the man might be an enemy combatant from Jericho, he asked, "Are you for us or for our enemies?" And the reply came, "Neither…but as commander of the army of the LORD I have now come" (Joshua 5:13-14).

Yes, this was the Lord saying, in effect, "I have not come to take sides; I have come to take over!" And that, ultimately, is the answer for those of us who lack courage: Jesus is not with us merely to help us; rather, He stands ready to fight for us, if only we will trust Him and let Him take charge.

On the tomb of Lord Lawrence in Westminster Abbey are the dates of his birth and death, along with an inscription that includes this statement:

> He feared Man so little,
> because he feared God so much.

Yes, if we fear God, we need fear nothing else.

With such confidence, like Joshua, we can walk into the unknown night with courage.

Taking God's Word to Heart

1. In the midst of great danger, Joshua stood strong, based on what God had told him. Today, believers can embrace the written Word of God. Share some promises from God's Word that provide you with strength in the midst of your current circumstances.

2. "Never will I leave you; never will I forsake you" (Hebrews 13:5) is one of the great promises of Scripture. What are some ways you can effectively apply the truths of this promise to your life of faith?

3. For what reasons might we, as Christians, be tempted to lack the courage to persevere, even though we know God is with us? How can you resolve such fears when you encounter them?

4. How can we reconcile the truth of God's presence in our lives with the reality that we as Christians can experience poverty, loneliness, the loss of loved ones, and other tragedies?

5. Consider the statement, "We live by promises, not explanations." How should that affect the way we perceive our difficult circumstances?

THE CROSS

1 Corinthians 1:18—*The message of the cross is foolishness to those who are perishing, but to us who are being saved it is the power of God.*

Galatians 6:14—*May I never boast except in the cross of our Lord Jesus Christ, through which the world has been crucified to me, and I to the world.*

The cross is widely misunderstood in our day. This can be proven by the fact that it is well nigh impossible to find anyone who will say anything bad about it. The cross is worn as a pendant by athletes, New Agers, and rock stars. This instrument of indescribable cruelty and shame is now a symbol of unity, tolerance, and spirituality of every kind. The true "message of the cross," as Paul put it, has long since vanished and has been largely replaced with a message reinterpreted to fit the modern mind. Many who wear the cross around their necks would be scandalized if they were to correctly understand its meaning.

Some, who want to be known as Christians, interpret the cross as the highest tribute to human value. They reason, "Because God was willing to send His Son to die for us, we must be of great worth as persons. Therefore we can use the cross as a means of affirming our dignity and bolstering our self-esteem." In this way they reason that people have a right to be blessed by God simply by virtue of who they are. Such a cross will not be an offense to anyone, nor would it be branded as foolishness. We are reminded of a sign seen on a vendor's table during a festival in Guatemala: *Cheap Crosses for Sale.*

The cross was not merely an instrument that had part in a cruel form of death. It deeply humiliated its victims; it was used to execute those who were most cursed. A crucifixion, with all of the torture that accompanied it, ended with the victim naked, with no rights, no reputation, and no recourse. Thus the cross not only proves the gracious love of God toward sinners, but also the depth of our sin and rebellion against Him. For us to love sin would be like loving the knife that was used to commit murder.

Jesus' suffering was terrible for the simple reason that our sin is terrible. And we must ever keep in mind that the suffering of Jesus was not primarily physical—it was not the lacerations, the crown of thorns, and the nails that hurt Him most. Rather, the spiritual suffering He endured—when His fellowship with the Father was broken for three hours on the cross—was the ultimate suffering He could possibly experience. It was the kind of agony we have never had to face.

Today it is often said that God forgives people on the basis of His love, rather than on the basis of an atoning sacrifice. Modern minds do not understand that God could not extend His grace toward sinners until His holy justice was completely satisfied. In order for God to redeem us, He needed the consent of all of His attributes. At the cross, God's inflexible holiness collided with His love, and the matter of salvation was accomplished to the mutual satisfaction of each. No wonder when we approach the cross we do so knowing that we are in the presence of a blessed mystery.

We cannot understand the cross unless we are prepared to grasp both its horror and its beauty. What happened to Jesus must be seen both as a crime to be condemned and an act of love to be admired. Most important, it must be seen as God's farthest reach; it is He who chose to come to our side of the chasm to redeem us. God did everything that needed to be done to make salvation possible.

No one can remain neutral at the foot of the cross. Either our devotion to Jesus will be rekindled or we will turn away, determined to take our own path. Let us bow in the presence of the cross with humility, worship, and gratitude, for it is here that we were redeemed for eternal glory.

Dietrich Bonhoeffer was right: "It is not before us but before the cross that the world trembles."

Taking God's Word to Heart

1. What comes to mind when you think of the cross? We've looked at 1 Corinthians 1:18 and Galatians 6:14; what other Bible passages teach us about the cross?

2. What is the central message of the cross? What key truths can we take from Christ's experience on the cross?

3. Reflect on the "depth" of the cross. Consider the depth of our sin, the depth of God's love, and the depth of Christ's sacrifice. Discuss as well the eternal significance of the cross.

4. Jesus endured both physical and spiritual suffering while on the cross. Most know of His physical suffering. What was so significant about His spiritual suffering?

5. In ways, the cross is a mystery to us. Why can no one remain neutral before the cross?

Note: This chapter was largely adapted from a portion of the book *Cries from the Cross*, by Erwin W. Lutzer (Chicago: Moody Press, 2002), pp. 14-25.

DISCERNMENT

Hebrews 5:14—*Solid food is for the mature, who by constant use have trained themselves to distinguish good from evil.*

Proverbs 3:5-7—*Trust in the LORD with all your heart and lean not on your own understanding; in all your ways submit to him, and he will make your paths straight. Do not be wise in your own eyes; fear the LORD and shun evil.*

Discernment is the ability to make a choice based on a biblical standard that honors God and edifies and benefits us and the people around us. Unfortunately, many Christians derive their standards of conduct from the culture that surrounds them. The clothes they wear, the movies they see, how they spend their money, and how they guide and train their children is influenced by society. They do whatever feels comfortable and imitate what others are doing without asking these basic questions: What does God say about this? What is His standard? They forget that we, as God's children, are called to a higher standard and a lifestyle that is very different from that of the world.

The influence and pressure from our decadent, sexualized society affects clothing styles, entertainment (movies, television, Internet), music, advertising, education, sports, recreation, travel, and pretty much everything else in life. Parents must be diligent and use discernment to help protect their children in as many ways as possible from the subtle evil that permeates the world around them. Don't be afraid to say no to friends, events, and things that conflict with a biblical standard.

Protect your children like a mother bear protects her cubs! Develop a focused and determined program to protect your children from anything that seeks to sexualize and demoralize their minds and bodies, deceive their hearts and affections, and turn their desires and ambitions away from knowing and pleasing God. This would include placing filters on the computers in your home, monitoring your children's activities and friends, and not allowing your children to have a television in their own bedroom.

We must pay attention to the instruction in 1 John 2:15-17, which says,

> Do not love the world or anything in the world. If anyone loves the world, love for the Father is not in them. For everything in the world—the lust of the flesh, the lust of the eyes, and the pride of life—comes not from the Father but from the world. The world and its desires pass away, but whoever does the will of God lives forever.

In that passage, the apostle John warns us about three things. The first is "the lust of the flesh"—that is, the forbidden sexual desires that cover a wide range of expressions: pornography, adultery, promiscuity, homosexuality, lust, and the like. The second is "the lust of the eyes," which means covetousness—that is, desiring what is not ours. The advertising industry knows that it can count on us to want what others have so they try to make us dissatisfied with everything from toothpaste to cars. The third is "the pride of life," which can be defined as self-love and absorption. To love the world is, at root, to worship the goddess of self—that is, our tendency to satisfy legitimate desires in the wrong way. When sin has control, pleasure through self-fulfillment and self-protection becomes our primary occupation.

Why is the love of the world so serious? If we love sin, we not only love what God hates, we love what put Jesus on the cross. To ask people, even those of us who follow Christ, to give up the sins that feed their desires is to ask for a battle. But if we want to become discerning Christians, we must constantly ask ourselves: Is this the kind of music I would listen to or the kind of movie I would watch if I had Jesus here for dinner? In 1 Corinthians 6:12 Paul said, "'I have the right to do anything,' you say—but not everything is beneficial. 'I have the right to do anything'—but I will not be mastered by anything."

Let us answer this question candidly: Are we in control of the entertainment we allow into our lives? Or are we driven, perhaps even obsessed, with the need for movies, TV shows, music, and the Internet? If something controls us, let us be honest enough to admit it and ask God for the strength and wisdom to control it.

Discerning Christians will take heed of this warning: "Be very careful, then, how you live—not as unwise but as wise, making the most of every opportunity, because the days are evil" (Ephesians 5:15-16). When Paul said we should make "the most of every opportunity," he used a Greek phrase that urges us to redeem the time—that is, we must buy the time out of the marketplace. There are so many demands for our time today that we have to make time for the things that matter to God.

Let us ask ourselves some hard questions: Are we satisfied with the way we spend our time? What kind of return are we getting on the number of hours we invest in watching television every week? Is the time spent making us a better person? Has it improved our character? Imagine what we would be like if we spent more time reading our Bible, praying, and becoming involved in the lives of others.

Someday we'll want to hear our Lord say, "Well done, my good servant!" (Luke 19:17). Each of us must make a decision of conscience: From what aspect of the world does the Lord want to free me? What am I loving that is damaging my devotion and affection for God and my commitment to my family?

As Christians—as those who bear light in the midst of a dark world—our greatest need is to live a righteous life and make sure our homes reflect a biblical standard. Without discernment, our lives will become crammed with the things that grieve God and hinder our fellowship with Him.

Taking God's Word to Heart

1. How would you define discernment as it pertains to your lifestyle? How do you determine what is clearly right and what is clearly wrong?

2. Give examples of how our values are often derived from contemporary culture, rather than from the Bible.

3. What are some ways parents can protect their children from the evil influences of the entertainment industry?

4. Based on 1 John 2:15-17, why is a love of the world so serious?

5. How can we do a better job of "redeeming the time" in these evil days?

ETERNAL LIFE

John 10:10—*The thief comes only to steal and kill and destroy; I have come that they may have life, and have it to the full.*

John 17:3—*Now this is eternal life: that they may know you, the only true God, and Jesus Christ, whom you have sent.*

1 John 5:11-12—*This is the testimony: God has given us eternal life, and this life is in his Son. Whoever has the Son has life; whoever does not have the Son of God does not have life.*

For the Christian, eternal life does not begin in eternity; eternal life is our present possession. In other words, it begins the moment we transfer our trust to Christ and receive Him as our personal Savior. Eternal life is a quality of life that is ours now to enjoy. It might be described as the enduring relationship we have with Christ, which explains why Jesus defined it as an intimate relationship with His Father. This relationship is established by the Holy Spirit the moment we are born again or given divine life.

Eternal life is not to be confused with eternal existence. Unbelievers will exist eternally in bodies that are fitted for the lake of fire, but they are never spoken of as having eternal life. In this life, unbelievers are described as physically alive but spiritually "dead in…transgressions and sins" (Ephesians 2:1). In contrast, eternal life refers to a quality of life that can be had only by those who have come to know the Father through faith in Christ.

When we trust Christ as our Savior, eternal life is given to us and we are transferred from the kingdom of darkness into the kingdom of light. We become a new creation, and "old things have passed away; behold, new things have come" (2 Corinthians 5:17 NASB). Thus, there is something within us that is created by God when we believe the gospel; there is a new nature within us that was not there before. We are spiritually raised from the dead and we become alive together with Christ.

What are the practical results of this gift of eternal life? In the here and now it motivates us to live differently, for we are "God's handiwork, created in Christ Jesus to do good works" (Ephesians 2:10). God births within us a love for Him and a desire to do His will.

Most importantly, we now can have the assurance of Christ's presence while we are here on earth. We can say, most humbly, that we have come to know the Father and enjoy fellowship with Him. His relationship with us is one of love and care. Having been embraced by Him, we will be His children throughout eternity.

Now that we have eternal life, we must learn to enjoy it. The apostle John wrote, "God is light; in him there is no darkness at all. If we claim to have fellowship with him and yet walk in the darkness, we lie and do not live out the truth. But if we walk in the light, as he [God] is in the light, we have fellowship with one another, and the blood of Jesus, his Son, purifies us from all sin" (1 John 1:5-7). Our most urgent assignment as believers is to develop a more intimate relationship with the Father day by day. As Jesus said, eternal life means that we know the Father.

The British preacher F.B. Meyer (1847–1929) was traveling on a train when an anxious and angry woman recognized him and shared her burden with him.

> For years she had cared for a crippled daughter who brought great joy to her life. She made tea for her each morning, then left for work, knowing that in the evening the daughter would be there when she arrived home. But

the daughter died, and the grieving mother was alone and miserable. Home was not "home" anymore.

This was the advice Dr. Meyer gave her: "When you get home and put the key in the door, say aloud, 'Jesus, I know You are here!' and be ready to greet Him directly when you open the door. And as you light the fire, tell Him what happened during the day; if anybody has been kind, tell Him; if anybody has been unkind, tell Him, just as you would have told your daughter. At night stretch your hand out in the darkness and say, 'Jesus, I know You are here!'"

Some months later, Meyer was back in the neighborhood and met the woman again, but he did not recognize her. Her face radiated joy instead of announcing misery. "I did as you told me," she said, "and it has made all the difference in my life, and now I feel I know Him."[2]

Contact with the beautiful Shepherd brings beauty into our scarred lives.

Physical death does not cut us Christians off from this divine life, but only leads us into a new existence and understanding of it. The life implanted by God within us today will lead to fellowship with Him throughout all of eternity. "Whoever has the Son has life; whoever does not have the Son of God does not have life" (1 John 5:12).

Everyone will live forever, but only those who have the Son have eternal life.

Taking God's Word to Heart

1. How do you define *eternal life*? What is said here about eternal life?

2. How are *eternal life* and *eternal existence* different?

3. How does one possess eternal life? (see 2 Corinthians 5:17). Describe the new nature within a believer. What is so significant about it?

4. Read Ephesians 2:10. What motivations does the prospect of eternal life provide for the Christian?

5. Knowing what you do about eternal life, what is your view of physical death?

FEAR OF THE LORD

Proverbs 1:7—*The fear of the LORD is the beginning of knowledge, but fools despise wisdom and instruction.*

Philippians 2:12-13—*Therefore, my dear friends, as you have always obeyed—not only in my presence, but now much more in my absence—continue to work out your salvation with fear and trembling, for it is God who works in you to will and to act in order to fulfill his good purpose.*

Should we fear the Lord today? Or is it safe to sin now that we are under grace?

Today, some Christians will tell you that we do not have to actually fear God because Jesus has borne the wrath of God for us. Because the judgment that should have come to us has fallen on Him, they would say that it is safe to sin. They go on to say that in Old Testament times, the fear of God was both commanded and proper, but in this era, on this side of the cross, we relate to God only in love, not fear. In fact, the impression is given that if a Christian fears God, he doesn't really understand the gospel, which has freed us from the penalties of the law. Love God, yes; fear Him, no.

Is it true that the fear of God is simply an Old Testament teaching or concept that disappeared with the coming of Christ? The decisive answer is no; the fear of the Lord is repeatedly commanded in the New Testament. For example, we read that the early church "increased in numbers, living in the fear of the Lord" (Acts 9:31). Peter said we should live our lives before God with "reverent fear" (1 Peter 1:17). God's holiness demands our fear.

Sometimes Bible teachers soften this clear teaching by saying that the word *fear* actually refers to reverence, not fear. But there is no reason to believe the New Testament writers were just speaking of reverence for God, though that, of course, is expected. The word *fear* in the New Testament has the same meaning as the various words used for *fear* in the Old Testament—the meaning is "to be afraid of." Yes, it is expected for us as Christians to be afraid of God, but as we shall see, it is a certain kind of fear.

Why should we fear God? First, because all sin has consequences, even for those who are believers. That's why Paul commands us to "continue to work out your salvation with fear and trembling" (Philippians 2:12). We often sing "Calvary Covers It All,"[3] and of course it is true that in Christ our sin has legally been taken away; but on a relational level, God disciplines His disobedient children. Just ask Ananias and Sapphira, whose lie cost them their lives (Acts 5:1-10). Even today the consequences of our sin result in damaged relationships, addictions, sorrow, and a wasted life. All sin—including our sins as Christians—have some immediate judgments. Unfortunately, many of us confuse the patience of God with the tolerance of God. "When the sentence for a crime is not quickly carried out, people's hearts are filled with schemes to do wrong" (Ecclesiastes 8:11).

Second, we should fear God because we know that our sin displeases Him. If we love God, we will not want to incur His displeasure. And when we offend Him and grieve the Holy Spirit, we should fear that our love of sin is greater than our love of God. And when we lose our fear of sin, we become the servant of sin and the consequences are out of our hands.

Of course, there is a wrong kind of fear of God. Even in the Old Testament there is a kind of fear that drives people away from God; but there is also another kind of fear that draws us toward God. When God appeared on Mount Sinai, the people of Israel were terrified, so

Moses made this interesting statement: "Do not be afraid. God has come to test you, so that the fear of God will be with you to keep you from sinning" (Exodus 20:20). Follow this carefully: On the one hand the people were not to tremble in fear, yet on the other hand, God had come to reveal Himself so they would fear Him and keep His commandments.

How do we explain this apparent contradiction? God was saying, "Do not fear Me as in the way of slaves, but rather fear Me as sons." The fear of a slave causes him to cower in the presence of his master. That is not the kind of fear we should have toward God. "Son fear" is something different—it motivates us to seek and please God.[4] Moses, who feared God as a son, went straight up Mount Sinai to pursue God more intensely. A proper understanding of the fear of the Lord motivates us to holiness (2 Corinthians 7:1). Jesus Himself took delight in the fear of the Lord (Isaiah 11:2-3). So there is a wrong kind of fear, and there is a kind of fear that is right and proper.

There is a sense in which both of us, as children, feared our fathers. As we were growing up, we knew that if we disobeyed our fathers, we would attract their displeasure. We never had the fear that our fathers would disown us, but we feared grieving them. That's how it is with our heavenly Father. The fear of the Lord is the beginning of wisdom because we who fear the Lord will be obedient to His will and will not want to displease the One who sent His beloved Son to redeem us. In fact, it's not possible to truly love God unless we also fear Him.

If we fear God, we need fear little else. When we properly fear the Lord, our lesser fears leave us. As we fear the Lord we will be convinced that ultimately God's opinion of us is the only one that really matters. Sinclair Ferguson writes, "To someone who fears God, His fatherly approval means everything, and the loss of it is the greatest of all griefs. To fear God is to have a heart that is sensitive to both His God-ness and His graciousness."[5]

Invite God to investigate all areas of your heart. Resolve with God's help to pursue the fear of the Lord, for it leads to blessings both now and forever. And if you have no fear of God, ask yourself why you have such a casual attitude toward the God who created the universe and chose you to be His child before the foundation of the world. Confess your lack of understanding of God's ways and seek Him with your whole heart.

Taking God's Word to Heart

1. What does it mean to fear the Lord?

2. We should fear God because our sins can bring immediate judgments. Consider the message of Ecclesiastes 8:11. What is the difference between the *patience* of God and the *tolerance* of God?

3. When we sin, we displease God. What are some possible consequences of incurring His displeasure?

4. Read Exodus 20:20. What does this verse teach?

5. What is the point of 2 Corinthians 7:1? What is son-fear? How did both Moses and Jesus exhibit son-fear?

FORGIVENESS

Ephesians 4:31-32—*Get rid of all bitterness, rage and anger, brawling and slander, along with every form of malice. Be kind and compassionate to one another, forgiving each other, just as in Christ God forgave you.*

Whatever you don't forgive, you pass on" a counselor wisely told a woman who bitterly complained about her unfaithful husband. Understandably, this woman was distraught, but when an offense festers in our hearts, we cannot confine it within our souls. Rather, it ends up spilling over into other relationships. Like burning incense in a dormitory, the smell cannot be confined to one room, but wafts down the hallway, into the washrooms, and all the way to the front door. Just so, our bitterness poisons personal relationships no matter how determined we are to keep it confined to a single room within our heart. Nursing an offense, quite literally, blinds us to our own faults, forces us to have skewed relationships, and warps our self-perceptions. Offended people often think they have a right to hurt others; after all, think of what *they* have been through!

How do we obey Paul's exhortation to forgive others as we have been forgiven? First, we must rejoice in the forgiveness that we ourselves have received. When God forgives us, He removes the barrier that sin placed between us and Him so that fellowship is restored. Jesus told a parable about a man who was forgiven his debt of what today would be millions of dollars, but he himself would not forgive a man who owed him perhaps fifty dollars (Matthew 18:21-35). The point, of course, is that the more aware we are of the enormity of our own sin that God freely forgave, the more inclined we are to show a willingness to forgive others.

Second—and this is difficult—we must be willing to surrender our attitude of "victimhood" and choose to never again be defined by what others have done to us. Some people keep their emotional wounds open, not wanting them to heal; they are like the boy who peeled his scab back to see if his wound was healing! For these people, their wounded past is their calling card, their perceived right to become manipulative, take advantage of others, and transfer their hatred to a mate or a child. Someone said of a married couple, "They buried the hatchet, but the grave was shallow and well marked." In other words, unless we are willing to give up our right to hold onto our wounds, we will always return to them when a crisis arises.

Third, we must take the wrong done to us and choose to give it to God in faith that He will "even the score" in His own time and in His own way. In the place of our wounds, we must substitute the wounds of Jesus; we must remember that He was wounded for us and therefore just as He bore the suffering that was our due, so should we accept the suffering that others have inflicted on us. So take your wounds and pour them out at the foot of the cross.

Finally, overcome any destructive thoughts you may have by replacing them with God's thoughts as found in His Word. Several years ago I (Erwin) was on a talk show with a man whose wife had experienced horrid abuse, and she, in turn, had abused others. After she was converted to Christ she memorized about 400 verses of Scripture that enabled her to put the past behind her so she could move on and help others. Today she has a credible ministry to those who have been emotionally damaged as she had been.

The result of our decision to forgive is that we will be compassionate, living with an attitude of forgiveness that marks us as one of God's children. As the saying goes, we are never more like humans when we are bitter and never more like God when we forgive. A grudge can become an idol in our hearts. The desire for vengeance can end up becoming more important to us than the willingness to obey God's command to forgive.

What offense is standing between you and your relationship with God? Is there something that someone did or some offense that cleaves to your soul? Spend time in God's presence and allow Him to show you that your idol of bitterness is sinful and destructive. Ultimately, the path to healing is to follow Christ's example: "When they hurled their insults at him, he did not retaliate; when he suffered, he made no threats. Instead, he entrusted himself to him who judges justly" (1 Peter 2:23).

God never intended that we bear the burden of the injustice we have experienced; He has promised to do that for us. Forgiveness is the only path toward restoring our relationship with God and freeing ourselves to do His will.

A Prayer for the Wounded

Father, will You go into the deepest places of my heart? Will You probe my conscience to reveal my sin? Will You pull the painful offenses out of my heart? Will You give me the strength to go to those whom I have wronged, or those who have injured me? Who, O Father, who is able to do these things? I cannot do them alone. Come to me at this moment. Set me free. I need Your help. I need to be broken and yielded. Grant to me all of these things, I ask. And don't stop working in me so that I can move beyond where I am at. In Jesus' name I pray. Amen.

Taking God's Word to Heart

1. What are the dangers of harboring bitterness, rage, and anger?

2. Paul teaches that we are to forgive others as we have been forgiven. To what is he referring? What steps are required on our part?

3. Each of us has been defiled by someone else. If we fail to willingly let the wounds heal, what results can we expect?

4. When wronged by another, how difficult is it to give that wrong to God by faith and substitute the wounds of Jesus for ours?

5. As we deal with forgiving others who have wronged us, a key to overcoming destructive thoughts that can poison our minds and hearts is to replace them with God's thoughts. What Scripture passages do you turn to when you need to forgive someone?

THE GLORY OF GOD

1 Corinthians 10:31—*Whether you eat or drink or whatever you do, do it all for the glory of God.*

2 Corinthians 3:18—*We all, who with unveiled faces contemplate the Lord's glory, are being transformed into his image with ever-increasing glory, which comes from the Lord, who is the Spirit.*

The word *glory* is a powerful word in the English language, and it immediately directs us to words such as *praise, worthiness,* and *honor.* In the Old Testament, the glory of God was an expression of His holiness. When God was with His people, His glory was visible; when He was grieved because of sin, the glory departed. The glory of God refers to His essence; it is the expression of His personal presence. Living for God's glory means that we bring honor to God by the responses we have to the circumstances of life. The crux of the issue is not whether we are able to avoid pain and suffering, whether we are rich or poor, happy or unhappy, but whether or not God is receiving glory from the faith we exhibit and our wholehearted devotion to Him. Our example, of course, is Jesus, who pleased not Himself, but was willing to endure the cross for the glory of God.

When the apostle Paul said we should eat and drink to "the glory of God," he was saying that all of life—even the mundane—is to be lived for the glory of God. In medieval times, many people thought that only works of a religious nature—such as saying a prayer or the giving of alms—was pleasing to God. But the great Reformer Martin Luther declared it isn't the action itself that pleases God, but rather the attitude of worship with which we carry out that action. That's what counts.

Elisabeth Elliot, whose husband was killed along with four other missionaries in Ecuador, later worked laboriously with an informant to break down a language into writing during a time when there were no photocopiers or computers. The suitcase in which she kept two years' worth of her translation work was stolen, and she had to begin the work all over again. When asked if she was angry about the theft that represented two years of hard work, she said, "No, this was my act of worship to God; what I did for Him was not lost." Now *that* is working for the glory of God!

When it comes to the difficulties of life, our first concern should not be how to reduce our pains or get circumstances that are more to our liking, but rather, how we can react in a way that honors God. Every morning before we get out of bed, we ought to pray, "O God, glorify Yourself in my life today at my expense!" Only when we are willing to pray that prayer have we finally agreed to live for the glory of God. And when we are willing to live with a single focus for the glory of God, we will discover that doing so helps reduce the stress in our lives. We will no longer find ourselves anxious about everything working out just right. Instead, we will accept—as coming from God's hands—those events that we can't control. And those things we can control, we are satisfied to do for God's good pleasure and glory.

In 2 Corinthians 3:18, the apostle Paul said the glory of God should be reflected in our lives: "We all, who with unveiled faces contemplate the Lord's glory, are being transformed into his image with ever-increasing glory, which comes from the Lord, who is the Spirit." Paul's point is that as we behold the glory of God, we are inwardly transformed to become more like Christ. We begin to love what we hated, and we come to hate what we loved. And we become more like Jesus. Obviously we cannot live this way without dying to our own ambitions and egos, and accepting God's sovereign right to do as He pleases with us.

The American writer Nathaniel Hawthorne wrote a story about some huge rocks on the side of a mountain that were thrown together in such a way that they resembled the face of a man. In the village across the valley, the villagers believed that someday, a person would appear whose face would resemble the Great Stone Face. Little Ernest, who grew up in the village, had a fascination for the face, and as a child, a teenager, and even as an adult he loved to sit and look across the valley at the Great Stone Face. He spent hours gazing at it.

Whenever a visitor came to the village, people would look to see if his face resembled the Great Stone Face. Poets and philosophers visited the village, but none resembled the Great Stone Face.

When he was an old man, Ernest addressed the village people, and as he spoke, they realized that his silhouette resembled that of the Great Stone Face. And they said, "Behold! Behold! Ernest is himself the likeness of the Great Stone Face!"

The lesson here is that *we become by beholding*. Our souls grow in relationship to what we gaze at, and so, as we look at Jesus, we become transformed into His image. Our focus is all-important. If we look at the things of this world, we'll become like the world. But if we behold the glory of the Lord, we will be transformed. We behold that glory through reading the Word and memorizing it. We behold it by worshiping with God's people, and letting the Word of God dwell richly in our hearts. The glory of God is all that matters.

Lord, glorify Yourself in our lives at our expense!

Taking God's Word to Heart

1. What does it mean for a Christian to live for God's glory?

2. In what ways is Jesus our example of living for God's glory? Drawing from the Gospel accounts, find two or three examples of Jesus' living His life for God's glory.

3. Read 1 Corinthians 10:31. What are some ways we can apply that verse to our lives?

4. How can we, in the midst of pain, suffering, and other difficult circumstances of life, live for God's glory?

5. As believers, we give glory to God as we are being transformed into His likeness. What is the key to becoming more
Christlike? Consider the examples of believers in whom you
see Christlikeness. In what specific ways are they having an
impact on others around them?

GOD

*Psalm 90:2—Before the mountains were born
or you brought forth the whole world, from
everlasting to everlasting you are God.*

*Romans 11:33—Oh, the depth of the riches of the
wisdom and knowledge of God! How unsearchable
his judgments, and his paths beyond tracing out!*

To say, "I believe in God" is a meaningless statement in our culture. The word *God* has become a canvas upon which people have felt free to paint their own portraits of the divine. For some, He is "psychic energy," and for others, He is an "inner power" that leads us into deeper consciousness. The list goes on and on. In short, people are turning God into whatever they want Him to be.

This raises an important question: From where should we derive our knowledge of God? There are only two possibilities. One is to begin with man and reason upward, but this only leads to an idolatrous conception that is little more than an enhanced image of ourselves. For the most part, our generation entertains ideas of God that are figments of the human imagination. God exists, in the minds of some, to flatter us, to approve of our conduct, and to satisfy our deepest desires. Tolerance is His dominant attribute.

The other way to understand God is to accept His revelation of Himself as given in the Bible. There we discover a God who not only is great but personal, and worthy of our submission and adoration. This

God is also meticulously holy and judges sin with severity. And, thankfully, He is also a God of grace who provided a way by which we may come to know Him.

Centuries ago, the great theologian Augustine said that the thought of God stirs us so deeply that we cannot be content without praising Him, "because you made us for yourself and our hearts find no peace until they rest in you." Before Augustine became a Christian, he was an immoral man. Thanks to the prayers of his mother, Monica, Augustine found himself reading the Scriptures, and he was soundly converted. He echoed the words of David: "As the deer pants for streams of water, so my soul pants for you, my God" (Psalm 42:1).

The Bible affirms that there is one God, creator of all things, holy, infinitely perfect, in whom all things have their source, support, and end. This God has limitless knowledge and sovereign power, and has graciously purposed from eternity to redeem a people for Himself and to make all things new for His glory. Because He is not limited in knowledge or power by any external forces or the will of His creatures, what He purposes will come to pass. To Him we owe the highest love, reverence, and obedience (Ephesians 1:3-5; 3:7-13; Revelation 4:11).[6]

Think for a moment about God having existed from all eternity. We can't get our minds around the concept, as the saying goes. And yet if we accept the basic proposition that "from nothing comes nothing," then God, of necessity, had to exist from all of eternity. If there had been a time when there was nothing, there would still be nothing today! Only a being that has always existed can account for the fact that something exists today. Yes, how true the Scriptures are when they affirm, "From everlasting to everlasting you are God."

Consider also God's wisdom and knowledge. He knows all things, both actual and possible. In other words, He not only knows what has happened in His universe; He also knows the details of what would have happened under different conditions. The staggering number of bits of information that comprise God's knowledge cannot be fathomed. Because He knows with unerring clarity the details of the past and He has an exhaustive knowledge of the future, it should be obvious that we can trust Him with all of our hearts.

The God of the Bible exists eternally in a loving tri-unity (trinity) of three equally divine Persons: the Father, the Son, and the Holy Spirit, each with distinct personal attributes, yet without division of nature, essence, or being (Deuteronomy 6:4; Matthew 28:18-20; Hebrews 1:1-3,8). And because God is a trinity, He can be a redeeming God.

The thousands of gods of Hinduism are worshiped, but do not claim to forgive sin. The god of Islam might be gracious to forgive his followers (though no one can be sure), but in so doing, his justice remains unsatisfied, for the sins he might choose to forgive are not atoned for. Buddhists do not believe in God, as such, but find themselves to be "one" with whatever exists, thus finding "god" within themselves.

Consider: The Bible teaches that "the person who sins will die" (Ezekiel 18:20 NASB). And because we are all sinners, we all must die, both physically and spiritually. No ordinary human being can die in our stead; we cannot make atonement for our own sin, much less for the sins of someone else. But if a perfect sacrifice were available—a perfect human being—whose offering was made acceptable to the Father, we could be redeemed.

Thus, in Christ, the God of the Bible became a human being—a sinless, perfect, divine human being—who would meet the requirements of justice that God the Father demanded. Thus He died in our stead so that we could be justly forgiven and accepted by God. His life, which was of infinite value, was adequate for all who would believe on Him.

Because God is a trinity, He was able to demand a sacrifice for our sins and then *supply what He Himself demanded*! All the meticulous standards of His holiness were duly met in Christ. Our responsibility and privilege is to accept what He has done for us. Such a God is worthy not only of our worship, but also our love and eternal gratitude.

No wonder that the doctrine of the one triune God is the glory of the Christian faith!

Taking God's Word to Heart

1. What does Genesis 1:1 tell us about the nature of God?

2. What are the two possible ways we can derive our knowledge of God? What contrasts can you draw between these ways?

3. What does the Bible tell us about God's attributes and character?

4. Try to explain why God, of necessity, had to exist from all of eternity.

5. The Bible teaches that God exists as a trinity. Read Deuteronomy 6:4; Matthew 28:18-20; and Hebrews 1:1-3,8. Briefly describe the Trinity. How is each member unique? What do we know about the function of each member?

6. What are some elements of Christianity that separate it from other world religions?

GRACE

Ephesians 2:8-9—It is by grace you have been saved, through faith—and this not from yourselves, it is the gift of God—not by works, so that no one can boast.

Grace is God's "unmerited favor" toward us; it comes to us as a gift we do not deserve. Here is something you can count on: The better you believe yourself to be, the less grace you will think you need. The more self-confident you are, the more convinced you will be that you could get by even if God were stingy with grace. All you need is some help from God and a bit of personal determination.

But our need is much more desperate, for grace finds us "dead in… transgressions and sins" (Ephesians 2:1). The fact God's grace alone is able to rescue us confirms that it is powerful enough and merciful enough to meet us where we are and bring us into the presence of God. "Because of his great love for us, God, who is rich in mercy, made us alive with Christ even when we were dead in transgressions—it is by grace you have been saved. And God raised us up with Christ and seated us with him in the heavenly realms in Christ Jesus" (verses 4-6).

Grace is given to us apart from anything we can do. Before salvation, we are dead in our sins. Our fallenness permeates our entire being: Our minds are tainted with sin, our souls are stained, and our wills are paralyzed. Good people or not, we are in deep trouble.

A newsman here in Chicago said that he is spiritually lost and someday he plans to do something about it. But Paul would say to him, "Not only are you unable to do something about it, but your very act of trying to do something about it will complicate the problem! Don't do anything about it until you have understood what God has done about it!" The newsman must receive what Christ has done about it, not what he thinks he is able to do about it.

Grace is a gift that sets aside all human merit. It does not simply give us a hand; it gives us a *resurrection*. Grace means that God takes the first step toward us. Then our small step of faith is simply a response to what God has already done. Grace means that God speaks a word, gives us spiritual life, and fits us to stand before Him. He descends the ladder we were trying to climb, scoops us up, and takes us all the way into His presence! Grace is all one-sided.

If God's rescue program had included our efforts, grace would be diminished and salvation would not be wholly the work of God. "And if by grace, then it cannot be based on works; if it were, grace would no longer be grace" (Romans 11:6). Some things can exist together, but the grace that brings salvation and human works cannot. Our self-effort will be put on a shelf labeled, "Unsuitable for Use." God acts alone because He does not need our cooperation. He invites us only to believe.

If you think that people are flocking to accept God's grace, not so. Intuitively, we think we have to have some part in our salvation, do some good work, or perform some deed that will make us worthy of God's grace. We compare ourselves with others and end up thinking we do not need God's grace because we are so good, or we reject God's grace because we believe ourselves to be too bad. Some people think to themselves, *If you knew what was in my past...you'd know that I've sinned too badly to accept God's grace.* They are convinced that God is so mad at them that no matter how much grace God extended, He would never accept them. They do not understand that their despair is intended to drive them *to* God rather than away from Him.

When you come to Christ you do not come to give, but to receive. You do not come to be helped, but to be rescued. You do not come just to be made better, though thankfully that does happen, but you come to be made alive! Nor do we make a promise; we come to believe *His* promise. It is His work and not our own that gives us the gift of grace.

Jesus told a story about two men who went into the temple to pray. The religious Pharisee prayed, "God, I thank you that I am not like other people—robbers, evildoers, adulterers—or even like this tax collector. I fast twice a week and give a tenth of all I get" (Luke 18:11-12).

If we think he was bragging, let's remember that he believed in a certain kind of grace. He thanked God that he was not like other men; he knew that his good works were done because of God's goodness toward him. I can just hear him saying, "But for the grace of God, there go I!" If he was better than others, God deserved the credit.

In contrast, the tax-gatherer who was nearby was so overwhelmed by his sin that he would not even lift his face to heaven. Instead, he beat his breast and said, "God, have mercy on me, a sinner" (verse 13).

Christ then said, "I tell you that this man, rather than the other, went home justified before God. For all those who exalt themselves will be humbled, and those who humble themselves will be exalted" (verse 14).

Yes, both men believed in God's grace. The self-righteous Pharisee thought that God's grace was needed only to do good deeds. God's grace, he thought, helps us do better.

The tax-gatherer saw God's grace differently. He knew that if he was to be saved, it would take a miracle that only God could do. He didn't just need help; he needed the gift of forgiveness, the gift of reconciliation. Only if grace were amazing could he be saved.

The Pharisee said, "God, if You help me, I'll do better and save myself!"

The tax-gatherer said, "God, You save me, or I'll damn myself!"

Those who think they can contribute to their salvation think that God's grace is wonderful; but only the humble who see themselves as God does believe His grace is amazing indeed. The difference is between those who know that God has to do it all and those who think they can help Him out.

No wonder that John Newton, who was a great sinner, knew he

needed special grace if he was to be forgiven. For him and for us, grace is truly amazing. Neither life on earth nor our stay in heaven will exhaust our wonder over God's grace.

> Amazing grace,
> How sweet the sound
> That saved a wretch like me!
> I once was lost, but now am found,
> Was blind, but now I see.[7]

Yes, grace is all one-sided. We bring nothing to God, except our sins. Grace is God's gift that gives us salvation.

Amazing indeed!

Taking God's Word to Heart

1. Why is the grace of God so important to mankind's sinful condition? Where does mankind fall short in trying to saving himself?

2. God's grace is a gift. How do we accept and take possession of it?

3. Read Romans 11:6. Why is it that God's saving grace and human works cannot coexist?

4. Read Jesus' parable in Luke 18:10-14. What is the point of this story?

5. Have we ever sinned so badly that we cannot accept God's gift of grace? Why?

GRIEF

1 Thessalonians 4:13—*Brothers and sisters, we
do not want you to be uninformed about those
who sleep in death, so that you do not grieve like
the rest of mankind, who have no hope.*

There is both bad grief and good grief. Bad grief paralyzes those who grieve and descends them into hopeless and unending despair; for such a person, grief is not a transition, but rather a destination. In contrast, good grief enables us to move along on our journey despite untold pain and loss. Or to put it differently: Bad grief stays in a tunnel with no light; good grief is in a tunnel but it sees light, or at least believes light exists.

A new widow who was very much in love with her husband met with me (Erwin) and confided that she had thought of suicide as a means to be reunited with him. She did not see how she could possibly live with the loneliness and deep longing to be with him; an unexpected heart attack had so cruelly severed their loving relationship. I told her she had but one responsibility, and that was to get up in the morning and make it through the day, and then repeat the process again and again for a year. I told her she could not retreat into her own cocoon, but had to continue her job and connect with other people, no matter how hard it was for her to do those things. I promised that although she might never get over her husband's death, "someday the sun will shine again." Years have now passed and yes, she tells me that I was right—the sun is shining again. We must say to all who are overcome with grief: "Life is always still worth living; there is still reason to hope."

We've known widows who have not wanted to move ahead even after years of grieving. They lacked the desire to re-enter a meaningful life and even felt that if they did, it would be disrespectful to the memory of their husband. Even our feelings themselves can become an idol when we insist that we will not surrender those feelings to God for our own good and for the good of those around us. It is wrong for any of us to worship the life we once had. Jan Glidewell was right: "You can clutch the past so tightly to your chest that it leaves your arms too full to embrace the present." [8]

Why do some people cleave to past relationships in unhealthy ways?

First, there is guilt. We know of a widow who went to the grave of her husband every day for 14 years, talking to her husband (though as a Christian she knew he wasn't listening) to ask forgiveness for insisting that they go to a concert together. He didn't want to go that evening, but she insisted, and en route, they were in a serious accident and he was killed. She could not get past the feeling that his death was her fault, never mind that she loved him and did not intend his death. This is, of course, false guilt. But it was this misguided sorrow that drove her to paralyzing grief that did not let her move on in her life. She was defined by her past relationship and could not embrace the present.

Second, there is self-pity—the kind that comes when one feels he has been so unfairly wronged by loss, while others more deserving of such a fate were spared. This feeling of undeserved loss can become so overwhelming that it eclipses all hope. A transition to a different life is neither desired nor imagined. Often this is accompanied by bitterness and anger because the tragedy seems so unfair.

We all can have an idolatrous attachment to the past that replaces faith in God and substitutes the memories of what once was. These memories can become all-consuming, and if they are combined with false guilt, they can hold us in emotional paralysis.

Here are some helpful insights from John Piper:

> *Enjoyment is becoming idolatrous when its loss ruins our trust in the goodness of God.* There can be sorrow at loss without being idolatrous. But when the sorrow threatens our confidence in God, it signals that the thing lost was becoming an idol.
>
> *Enjoyment is becoming idolatrous when its loss paralyzes us emotionally so that we can't relate lovingly to other people.* This is the horizontal effect of losing confidence in God. Again: great sorrow is no sure sign of idolatry. Jesus had great sorrow. But when the desire is denied, and the effect is the emotional inability to do what God calls us to do, the warning signs of idolatry are flashing.[9]

Paul says we should grieve, but not without hope. Jesus wept at the tomb of Lazarus, and also wept over the city of Jerusalem. We have good reason to grieve when we experience loss—whether the loss of a friend or of a coveted opportunity. In fact, those who don't appropriately grieve are out of touch with their emotions, and perhaps even harbor a callous disregard for themselves and others.

A good kind of grief helps us to transition from where we now are to where we should be.

Taking God's Word to Heart

1. Contrast "bad" grief with "good" grief. What are the results of both kinds of grief?

2. All of us have experienced (or will experience) grief due to the loss of a loved one. How have you dealt with grief? Were you able to channel your emotions in positive ways to encourage others?

3. How does guilt deter us from getting beyond a past relationship? Why do we call it false guilt?

4. Another deterrent to moving beyond past relationships is self-pity. In what ways does self-pity undermine us?

5. Idolatrous attachments to the past that replace our faith in God can be crippling. Reread John Piper's insights from his book *Discerning Idolatry in Desire*. What lessons can we learn here?

HEAVEN

Revelation 21:1-3—*I saw "a new heaven and a new earth," for the first heaven and the first earth had passed away, and there was no longer any sea. I saw the Holy City, the new Jerusalem, coming down out of heaven from God, prepared as a bride beautifully dressed for her husband. And I heard a loud voice from the throne saying, "Look! God's dwelling place is now among people, and he will dwell with them. They will be his people, and God himself will be with them and be their God."*

What can we expect to experience in heaven?

In heaven we will be with Jesus; we will become reacquainted with our friends and relatives, and then we will adjust to a new life in an entirely different realm. We will discover that our bodies are able to travel horizontally and vertically without any effort, with speed and grace.

Then what?

Someone has said that for us to speak about what life will be like in heaven is like two infants in a womb talking about what their life will be like between birth and reaching the age of 20! Yet the Bible gives us enough information to imagine and even speculate about what we can expect in the blessed life to come.

There are some things we will *not* find in heaven: There will be no tears, no death, no crying, no pain, and no curse. Also, there will be no temple there, "because the Lord God Almighty and the Lamb are its temple. The city does not need the sun or the moon to shine on it, for the glory of God gives it light, and the Lamb is its lamp" (Revelation 21:22-23).

No temple? In the Old Testament, before the temple was built, the people of Israel had the tabernacle. It was basically comprised of three areas: the outer court; the holy place, which the priests could freely enter; and the inner room known as the Holy of Holies, where the glory of God was revealed. Only the high priest could enter this room, and he could do so only one day a year—on the Day of Atonement.

The Holy of Holies was the shape of a cube, and so is our future holy city, the New Jerusalem (verses 16-17). There will be no need of a tabernacle or temple because the entire New Jerusalem is the Holy of Holies! In other words, we will live forever in the immediate presence of God.

Joni Ereckson Tada, an author and speaker who has been quadriplegic for more than 40 years, says that what she anticipates most about heaven, is not a new body with new legs so that she can run toward Jesus; rather, she looks forward to enjoying God without sin ever intruding into their relationship! Imagine having thoughts so pure and holy that we will not mind if anyone could clearly see what we were thinking! In heaven, we will experience total purity and unhindered, two-way fellowship with God.

What about our privileges in heaven? There will be true equality, for even the kings of the earth will surrender their glory to the reigning Christ (verse 24). Also, we will enjoy perfect health, for we will finally be able to eat from the tree of life. And we are told that "the leaves of the tree are for the healing of the nations" (22:2). Of course we will not eat in heaven because we *have* to, but like the resurrected Jesus, who ate fish with His disciples on the shore of Galilee, we will eat for sheer enjoyment and fellowship.

And what will we do in heaven? In a *The Far Side* cartoon, the artist drew a picture of the stereotypical view of heaven: a man with angel wings playing on his harp, with a bored look on his face, saying, "I wish I had brought a magazine!" Wrong—in heaven, no magazines are needed!

We will be busy serving Christ and we will reign with Him "forever and ever" (22:5). We can't imagine what this means, but we might even be asked to explore other planets and exercise authority over realms now unknown. But it's clear we will be eternally busy, doing the Master's will and loving every moment of it.

The Bible begins in a garden and ends in a city. The reason for a city with walls and gates is not to keep uninvited people out. Indeed, we read that the gates of the city are never closed. The reason we will live in a city is to foster community; we will meet as we go outside the gates and we will congregate on the city's main street, where God's throne is forever established. Our fellowship will not just be with God, but with the saints of all the ages, and with all who have come to trust Him for salvation and grace. You'll get to spend as much time as you like with Abraham and Peter—there's no rush, we have all of eternity.

John was limited in the description he gave about the New Jerusalem because human language can only say so much. Heaven will be more beautiful than anything we could ever imagine; what we will see and experience there are beyond the limits of present thought. What's more, we can unpack our bags for the last time ever because we are there to stay. Forever is a long time!

One evening a mother read stories about Jesus to her little daughter, who dreamed of Jesus that very night. In the morning, she said to her mother, "I dreamed about Jesus and He is so much more beautiful than the pictures in the book!"

"He who testifies to these things says, 'Yes, I am coming soon.' Amen. Come, Lord Jesus. The grace of the Lord Jesus be with God's people. Amen" (Revelation 22:20-21).

Taking God's Word to Heart

1. Do you often reflect on what heaven will be like? What are you most looking forward to when you arrive?

2. The Bible does provide interesting information about heaven. What kind of body will we have there? How will our bodies function differently?

3. We are accustomed to so many things associated with this earthly life. Read Revelation 21:22-23. What things will we *not* find in heaven? What new experiences await us there?

4. According to Scripture, what sort of privileges will we enjoy in heaven?

5. The Bible tells us that we will serve Christ "for ever and ever" (Revelation 22:5). What all that involves may be up to speculation at this point. What do you envision we might do that could keep us eternally busy?

HELL

Luke 12:5—*I will show you whom you should fear: Fear him who, after your body has been killed, has authority to throw you into hell. Yes, I tell you, fear him.*

Revelation 20:15—*Anyone whose name was not found written in the book of life was thrown into the lake of fire.*

The doctrine of hell has all but disappeared from our churches. Because it offends our sensibilities we are tempted to ignore it, reinterpret it, or otherwise discount it. Yet the Bible not only repeatedly teaches the doctrine of hell; it also describes a terrifying judgment when multitudes stand before the throne of God unprepared. And all who appear at this judgment will be "thrown into the lake of fire."

Let's answer some questions about this judgment: Who is on that throne? And, who are the defendants standing in line? And on what basis will they be judged? And, finally, what do we know about the lake of fire, and is it a just punishment? Before reading further, you'll want to take a moment to open your Bible and read the description of this event in Revelation 20:11-15.

Who is on this majestic throne? We can be sure that it is Jesus, for the Scriptures teach that God has "entrusted all judgment to the Son" (John 5:22). This Jesus, the baby of Bethlehem, so loved at Christmastime but ignored during the rest of the year, is now the judge of all the unredeemed. His throne is great, majestic, and being white, signifies His holy justice and impartiality.

In Revelation 20:12 John wrote, "I saw the dead, great and small, standing before the throne." How did these people get here? They were summoned from all parts of the world, raised from the dead to give an account to God. John said that even "the sea gave up the dead that were in it" (verse 13). The ancients believed that if you died at sea or if you were cremated and your ashes thrown into the sea, then the gods could never find you, so you need not fear an afterlife. But God will finds the bodies of all mankind—bodies long since disintegrated in ages past, bodies eaten by sharks or lost in the rubble of an earthquake. God knows the location of every particle of matter in the universe, and thus is able to summon these bodies to appear before Him.

And, of course, these bodies will be joined with their souls, which is why John wrote, "Death and Hades gave up the dead that were in them" (verse 13). Hades is the present abode of the souls of all unbelievers who have died in the past and will die in the future. When God calls upon these people to judge them, their souls in Hades will be joined with their resurrected bodies fitted for eternity, bodies fitted for the lake of fire.

The great and small will be there: the kings will stand among slaves; the rich will stand with the poor; the religious zealots will stand with the atheists. No doubt people of all religions will be represented—Protestants, Catholics, Hindus, Muslims, and so on.

On what basis will they be judged? A book will be opened that details all their works—all the words they have ever spoken, all the secrets of their hearts, and of course all the lies they spoke in an attempt to cover these secrets! Basically, God will judge everyone on the basis of what they did with what they knew. Those who did not know the gospel will be judged by their own conscience and the light gleaned from nature. This judgment will show that no one has lived up to what they intuitively or rationally knew to be right.

Jesus said that it will be more tolerable in the day of judgment for Sodom and Gomorrah than for those cities that rejected Him when He was on earth (Matthew 10:11-15). Clearly, those who heard the gospel and rejected it, and those who had greater access to the gospel (as is the case in North America), will be judged more strictly. To the pagan who has never heard of Christ, God will not say, "You will be thrown into the lake of fire because you didn't believe in Jesus." Rather, God will judge that person on the basis of what he did with what he knew. As M.R. DeHaan wrote, "Hell for the pagan headhunter who has never heard the Word of God is going to be heaven compared to what it will be for those who have heard the pleading of the gospel and rejected it."[10]

Those who did evil will be given a lesser punishment than those who not only did evil but also enticed others to do the same. For example, Jesus said this about those who cause "little ones" to sin: "It would be better for them to be thrown into the sea with a millstone tied around their neck than to cause one of these little ones to stumble" (Luke 17:2).

Everyone who stands before God in this judgment will fall short, for they will lack the one requirement needed to enter heaven. Because their names are not in the Book of Life (that is, the book of the redeemed), they will be cast into the lake of fire. They had never experienced the forgiveness of God; their hope was not in Christ, who alone is qualified to give us the righteousness God accepts.

Is this judgment unjust? We could argue that these people did wrong, but after all, they were born sinners along with the rest of us. Doesn't condemning people to eternal punishment fly in the face of common human compassion and fairness? Well, think of it this way: What if, as Jonathan Edwards said, the greatness of a sin is determined by the greatness of the being against whom it is committed? To throw a snowball at a mailman is one thing; to throw one at a policeman is another. And to throw a snowball at the president of the United States will get you arrested. Using that analogy, think of the infinite crime of sinning against an infinite God. Sin is much more serious to God than it is to us. Also, because we are created as eternal beings, those who are sent to the lake of fire will bear the consequences of their personal guilt forever. They will forever remain the objects of God's anger toward sin.

It comes down to this: God is repeatedly described in the Scriptures as meticulously just. We honor Him by believing and trusting in His justice, knowing that someday we will agree with all of His decisions and forever sing, "Just and true are your ways, King of the nations" (Revelation 15:3). I have no doubt that those who are in the lake of fire will agree that they are being justly punished because their sin will be present to their minds and consciences. That in itself will be a form of hell.

The doctrine of hell is a difficult one to talk about. But we cannot avoid it. It is present in Scripture, and Christ frequently warned the lost about hell out of great compassion for them—a compassion we should share as well.

Taking God's Word to Heart

1. What does the Bible teach us about hell?

2. Describe the scene at the throne of judgment. What is the purpose of this event?

3. Read Revelation 20:11-15. This passage speaks of a judgment. Who is judged? How is the judgment played out?

4. On what basis will Jesus judge the multitudes? What will this judgment prove?

5. Will Jesus' judgments be just? Is an eternal punishment a fair judgment?

THE HOLY SPIRIT

John 7:37-39—*On the last and greatest day of the festival, Jesus stood and said in a loud voice, "Let anyone who is thirsty come to me and drink. Whoever believes in me, as Scripture has said, rivers of living water will flow from within them." By this he meant the Spirit, whom those who believed in him were later to receive. Up to that time the Spirit had not been given, since Jesus had not yet been glorified.*

Galatians 5:22-23—*The fruit of the Spirit is love, joy, peace, forbearance, kindness, goodness, faithfulness, gentleness and self-control. Against such things there is no law.*

Adoniram J. Gordon, one of the founders of Gordon-Conwell Divinity School, told of a time when he looked across a field and saw what he thought was a man pumping water. The man appeared to be pumping effortlessly and continually. As Gordon walked closer, he discovered that it wasn't a man pumping water, but rather, a wood figure painted to look like a man. In fact, this figure wasn't pumping water at all—it was attached to a pump mechanism, and an artesian well was creating the energy to turn the mechanism that caused the figure to move. Rather than pumping water, the figure was actually being pumped by water from the well!

Jesus likened the gift of the Holy Spirit to a well of living water, which He said would spring up within us and lead to eternal life. Like water to parched ground, the Holy Spirit offers refreshment and help to our weary souls. Jesus offers this water in abundance to all who are thirsty and willing to come to Him and drink.

Just read Jesus' invitation at the Jewish Feast of Tabernacles: "On the last and greatest day of the festival, Jesus stood and said in a loud voice, 'Let anyone who is thirsty come to me and drink. Whoever believes in me, as Scripture has said, rivers of living water will flow from within them'" (John 7:37-39).

Jesus promised not merely a stream, but streams. All who drink will have their own artesian well within them. He calls with a loud voice to all who are weary of empty religion, to all who are weary of worldly pursuits.

This gift of the Spirit is given to the thirsty: "Let anyone who is thirsty." Those who are spiritually thirsty know the difference between being satisfied with God and seeking satisfaction from the empty watering holes of the world. Tragically, some think they are not thirsty because they eke out a bit of satisfaction from the stagnant streams of sensuality and personal ambition. They do not know that they were born with a raging thirst that only Jesus can satisfy.

The woman who encountered Christ at the well had been married five times and was living with a sixth man who was not her husband. She could neither depend on a husband nor her friends for comfort and hope. But Christ offered her living water that would spring up to eternal life (John 4:14). He offered inner resources that would bring cleansing to her troubled conscience and help her cope with the pain of her failed marital relationships.

Jesus introduced the ministry of the Holy Spirit to His disciples before His death. They had come to depend on Jesus for everything, and when He announced that He was leaving them, they felt abandoned. Jesus would not be with them to answer their questions, to teach them, or to offer solutions to the challenges of their daily lives. They had come to love Him deeply, and they knew His absence would be keenly felt.

Jesus gave them this reassurance: "I will ask the Father, and he will give you another advocate to help you and be with you forever…I will not leave you as orphans; I will come to you" (John 14:16,18). The disciples would not be orphaned; in fact, thanks to the gift of the Spirit, Jesus in effect promised, "I'll be closer to you than I've ever been before." That promise was fulfilled by the gift of the Spirit, the third Person of the Trinity.

What is your need today? Is it for companionship? The Holy Spirit is with you. Is it for comfort? The Holy Spirit stands ready to help. Do you need an advocate? He is ready to plead your case. And, if your sorrow is so deep that you do not know how to pray, the Holy Spirit will intercede with groaning that is too deep for words (Romans 8:26).

Many Christians entertain false ideas about the Holy Spirit. For example, there are those who think that the Spirit indwells only some Christians but not others. Be assured that all Christians are indwelt by the Holy Spirit (Romans 8:9; 1 Corinthians 6:19). The indwelling Spirit seals us until the day of redemption and is a guarantee that we are God's children, assuring us that we will be taken safely to heaven (Ephesians 1:14; 5:30). However, we will not experience the Spirit's life and power if we grieve Him with sin that we are neither willing to confess nor forsake.

Although all believers are *indwelt* by the Spirit, not all believers are *filled* with the Spirit. To be filled with the Spirit means that we are experiencing the Holy Spirit's gentle guidance and control in our lives. To be filled with the Spirit means that the Spirit is reproducing His fruit within us. We should never think that the filling of the Spirit is just for those Christians who are the spiritually elite. I like to tell people that the Spirit is not given only to those who "have it all together," but to the rest of us so that we might be able to "get it all together." But for us to enjoy the Spirit's ministry, we must meet some basic conditions.

We are warned to keep our temple clean through confession of sin and submission to God (1 Corinthians 6:19). Our bodies are the temple of the Holy Spirit, and He wants the key to the hidden closets of our hearts. We must not grieve the Spirit by allowing conditions to develop in our hearts that force the Holy Spirit to coexist with unconfessed sin. No one can exaggerate the suffering the Holy Spirit experiences when living in a temple that is unclean. He is grieved because He loves us and knows the damage sin does in our lives. When He is grieved, He does not feel at home in our hearts; His ministry to us is quenched.

To experience the Spirit's fullness, we also need faith. A preacher of another era, F.B. Meyer, told how desperately he sought the filling of the Holy Spirit. He knew he was indwelt by the Spirit, but he could not seem to receive the Spirit's help for ministry. He said he left a meeting and was walking wearily through the night praying, seeking what he lacked. He said, in esssence, "Lord, if there is anyone who needs the filling of the Spirit, it is I. But I am too tired, too nervously run down to agonize, too weary to tarry, and yet I need the Spirit's refreshment so desperately."

Then he said it was as if he heard a voice saying, "As you took forgiveness from the hands of the dying Christ, so you may take the refreshment of the Spirit from the hands of the ascended Christ." Then in simple faith, he said, "I then took for the first time and have been taking ever since." We receive the benefits of the cross by faith; we also receive the benefits of the ascension by faith—namely, the fullness of the Spirit.

Years ago when archaeologists entered the ancient pyramids in Egypt, they discovered grain that was 4000 years old. Yet incredibly, when they planted the grain, it grew! The life within the grain was present during those centuries, but it did not have the proper conditions to sprout. In warm sunshine and moist soil, the hard shell softened and the life began to grow. When the water of the Spirit and the sunshine of God's Word come together in our lives, the result is that the life of the Spirit begins to become active within us.

Today the Holy Spirit invites us, saying, in effect, "I will develop a close relationship with you; I will help you to walk; I will help you to cope; I will help you through your trial; I will refresh your spirit." This invitation is for all who have come to know Christ personally. Are you willing? The Spirit is!

No one who has ever walked through a desert says, "One good drink of water is enough for the week!" No, when you are trekking through the desert you need water daily, hourly. When the nineteenth-century evangelist D.L. Moody was asked why he had to be filled with the Spirit so often, he said simply, "Because I leak."

How often do we have to drink of the Spirit? As often as we thirst; as often as we have a need; as often as we leak. Let us come to Christ, not with a cup but with a bucket—believing that He will give us the refreshment He promised.

Taking God's Word to Heart

1. What is the gift of the Holy Spirit? Why did Jesus send the Spirit to us?

2. What is the thirst that the "springs of living water" quenches? Contrast the springs of living water with the watering holes of the world. Why do the world's methods for quenching our spiritual thirst never satisfy?

3. As believers, in what specific ways do we benefit from the ministry of the Holy Spirit?

4. Read 1 Corinthians 6:19. Because the believer's body is the temple of the Holy Spirit, what is the believer's responsibility? What causes the Spirit to grieve?

5. What is the key to a believer experiencing the Spirit's fullness?

HOPE

Romans 8:28—*We know that in all things God works for the good of those who love him, who have been called according to his purpose.*

Romans 15:13—*May the God of hope fill you with all joy and peace as you trust in him, so that you may overflow with hope by the power of the Holy Spirit.*

Where do you go when the days are dark and the nights are long, and when you suffer unexpected loss or unbearable pain? Hope is found in Romans 8:28. This awesome promise doesn't enable us to see exactly *why* God lets events happen as they do, nor is it a quick cure for sorrow, but it is a promise we can cling to because we know that God is working things out toward our good.

Recently we attended the funeral of a friend who had a very rare form of cancer. He died at age 64. We did not say to his grieving widow and children, "Dry your tears now because all things work together for good to them who love God," because that would have been insensitive and hurtful. But still, his dear widow will find much solace in these words as the days go by.

This promise is given only to those who love God, and those who are called according to His purpose. When God calls us to Himself, we are converted, and He creates within our hearts a supernatural love for Himself.

We also have the assurance that this promise is true. Paul began Romans 8:28 with the words, "We know…" We can have a deep and settled assurance, given by the Holy Spirit, that this promise is true and reliable. We can know it is true not because we see it with our own eyes, but because we believe in the care of a loving, sovereign God.

The words "all things" in Romans 8:28 means that *everything* works together for good. Life is haphazard with no neat categories, but God makes everything fit together. He uses righteous things such as His people and His Word. He uses negative things such as sickness, the loss of a loved one, financial reversals, and even abuse and divorce. This means that God is able to take what is intended for evil, and even our enemies, and work them out for our ultimate good. It does not mean that everything that happens is good, but that God will make everything work together for good.

God even uses the sins that we commit to bring about something good. Don't misunderstand. Sin is never justified, and if we sin so that grace will abound, we will be disciplined for our disobedience. But yes, God is able to take our sin and use it in ways that we cannot even imagine. He can use our sin to help us see ourselves more clearly and realize our great need for Him. In the end, when we repent, we can then be drawn closer to God than ever. Psalm 119:67 says, "Before I was afflicted I went astray, but now I obey your word."

You may be thinking, *Can God really make evil, sin, false accusations, injustice, broken relationships, cruelty, betrayal, hatred, jealousy, and abandonment work together for good?* The answer is *yes* because Jesus experienced all of these things in His last hours. Calvary is the quintessential example of how God can take something that is thoroughly and entirely evil and through it display His grace. He used Calvary both for our good and His glory. Wicked hands crucified Christ, and His enemies will be thoroughly judged for what they did, yet our salvation came from the cross. That is supreme proof that good can come out of evil.

Paul said that all things "work for the good." The Greek term used here is *sunergeo*, from which is derived the English word *synergism*, which has to do with the working together of different agents "such that the total effect is greater than the sum of the individual effects."[11] *Soon* means "together" and *ergo* means "to work." God works, and He works things together. God knows the outcome in ways that you and I cannot possibly fathom, and He works things together for good.

Have you ever taken the back off of an old clock? Some of those little wheel-shaped gears go in the same direction as the hands, while other gears turn counterclockwise. Some turn more quickly, while others move slowly. Looking only at the mechanisms, you'd get the impression that some of those tiny gears were working against what the clock was trying to accomplish. But when you look at the clock's face and note that it is keeping time accurately, you would agree that all the parts are working together as a whole for good.

With that in mind, when you have a bad day, it may be a very good day from God's standpoint. God is synergizing the events of your life so that over time, they work together for good. The promise in Romans 8:28 teaches that by His power and grace God weaves, overrides, and makes events converge in such a way that that good can be brought out of human tragedy.

A pastor's son committed suicide. After an absence of several weeks from the pulpit, the pastor returned and read Romans 8:28 to his congregation, and said, "It is impossible for me to see how any good can come of my son's death, yet I realize I see only a part," and then he spoke about what he called the miracle of the shipyard.

He said, "A modern ship is made mostly of steel. If you put any individual part into the ocean it will sink. However, because of how all the parts are put together, when the last rivet is put in place, the ship floats—against all odds." Then he said, "Taken by itself, my son's suicide is senseless. Throw it into the sea of Romans 8:28 and it sinks. I can see no good in it. But when the master shipbuilder is finally finished, even this tragedy will be built together in a way as to serve God's unsinkable purpose."

What faith!

No wonder Paul referred to God as "the God of hope" in Romans

15:13. He connected this hope with personal joy and peace, and invites us to overflow with hope by the power of the Holy Spirit. For the Christian, there are plenty of tragedies, but they're never permanent. For the non-Christian there are no permanent triumphs. If you don't love God, you are *not* called according to His purpose, and the promise in Romans 8:28 doesn't apply to you. You may exist for God's good, but you will never exist for your own good ultimately.

For those who know God, hope abounds. Those who know the Savior can rest their head on the pillow of a hope that cannot be suppressed. No tragedy is permanent—and there is no heartbreak that will not be healed.

This is a promise you can believe in.

Taking God's Word to Heart

1. Read Romans 8:28. What does this verse mean to you? Why do you think believers cling to this promise?

2. To what does "all things" refer? Does this include both good and bad things? What is God able to do with the bad things?

3. What evil things were done to Christ in the hours leading up to His crucifixion and death? Compare that seemingly hopeless scenario with the victory of the cross.

4. What is the significance of the phrase "work together"? Recall an instance in your life where God took a bad situation and orchestrated a good result. Had you lost hope before God was finished?

5. In Romans 15:13, Paul connects hope with joy and peace. "That you may overflow with hope" is a powerful action linked to the power of the Holy Spirit. What does this overabundance of hope mean to the Christian during the course of life?

JESUS

John 1:1—*In the beginning was the Word, and the Word was with God, and the Word was God.*

John 14:6—*Jesus answered, "I am the way and the truth and the life. No one comes to the Father except through me."*

Who is Jesus, and why does it matter?

Understanding who Jesus is leads us directly into the heart of Christianity. When the apostle John said that in the beginning was the Word and "the Word was God," he was affirming what is taught throughout the New Testament: Jesus is God. In fact, if He were not God, He could not be our redeemer.

For our part, everything we do is tainted with sin. Even when we do good things, our motives are often mixed with self-interest and pride. Because God is holy, He cannot accept our good deeds, no matter how well intentioned, as a basis for accepting us. If we are to be saved from our sins, God alone is going to have to do the saving. Because God is just, an adequate penalty had to be offered for our sins; someone had to die in our place. No ordinary man could make such a sacrifice for all of us; no human being with a sin nature could possibly meet God's standard of absolute perfection.

God operates by a basic principle: All sin, if it is to be forgiven, demands a sacrifice to pay the penalty we deserve. Blood has to be shed. If someone has to be justly punished for our sins, and if no ordinary human can qualify, then God Himself has to supply the offering for our sins. God Himself must do what we can't.

Obviously, it is not possible for God, who is spirit, to be nailed to a cross and suffer as our substitute. In Jesus, God became a man so He could be our redeemer, doing what no ordinary man could ever do. Jesus, as the second member of the Trinity, paid the penalty for all who would believe on Him; this sacrifice was made to God the Father, who accepted it and raised Jesus from the dead as proof of His triumph.

Jesus alone has the qualifications to be our Savior. Prophets, gurus, and other religious teachers are themselves sinners, unable to save themselves, much less anyone else; they are teachers, not saviors. Jesus was entirely sinless, not a part of our predicament, and hence qualified to lift us from where we are and take us to where we need to be—namely, in the presence of His Father.

This explains why those who deny the divinity of Jesus deny the gospel. If Jesus were not God, He would not be able to help bridge the chasm that separates God and man. He would be like a bridge that is broken at the farthest end. He would be disqualified to do what needed to be done. Thankfully, as the God-man He purchased redemption for us.

This helps explain why Jesus said that no one could come to the Father except through Him. No other person has the ability to justly forgive our sins and then bless us with the only kind of righteousness God the Father accepts—namely, divine righteousness. And this gift is given freely to those who believe on Him as Savior. We are reminded of the words of the angel spoken to Joseph while he was betrothed to Mary: "She will give birth to a son, and you are to give him the name Jesus, because he will save his people from their sins" (Matthew 1:21).

When a Roman emperor decided it was time for the persecution of Christians to stop, he thought he would do them a favor by putting a statue of Jesus in the Roman Pantheon alongside all the Roman gods. But the Christians objected, saying in effect, "You are not doing us a favor by adding Jesus to the gods of Rome; He must stand alone as King of kings and Lord of lords."

Through the ages since His crucifixion and resurrection, the life of

Jesus has been studied and dissected; He has been praised and vilified, believed and ridiculed. But of this we can be sure: Those who accept Him as the Son of God have discovered He is as good as the promises He made. He can be trusted to give the eternal life that He offers to all who believe on Him.

Who is Jesus? God in the flesh.

And why does it matter? He alone is able to redeem us.

Taking God's Word to Heart

1. What basic New Testament truth does John 1:1 confirm?

2. Nothing we can do as humans will meet God's standard of absolute perfection. What qualifies Jesus to be our Savior?

3. When it comes to punishment for sin, by what principle does God operate?

4. What does the resurrection of Jesus signify to the world?

5. In John 14:6, Jesus says that "no one comes to the Father except through me." What does that statement mean to a person needing forgiveness of his or her sins?

JUSTIFICATION

Romans 5:1—*Therefore, since we have been justified through faith, we have peace with God through our Lord Jesus Christ.*

Romans 8:33-34—*Who will bring any charge against those whom God has chosen? It is God who justifies. Who then is the one who condemns? No one. Christ Jesus, who died—more than that, who was raised to life—is at the right hand of God and is also interceding for us.*

How perfect do you have to become to be welcomed into heaven? "I hope not too perfect," a friend of ours answered. "If I have to be perfect, I just won't make it!" He was hoping that God would be lenient—*very* lenient!

We surprised him by saying that he did indeed have to be perfect—as perfect as God. As he thought about it, he realized it made sense that God, who is holy, cannot accept us unless we are as perfect and holy as He Himself is.

So the question before us—the question that goes to the heart of what we call the gospel—is this: How do we become as perfect as God?

There are some people who think that Martin Luther was a turncoat, a confused man who was angry at the church of his time for petty, personal reasons. Well, we're not going to defend everything that Luther did or wrote, but we believe that more than anyone else of his day, he grappled with the question of how a sinner can receive the favor of God—a God who isn't lenient and hates sin.

While preparing a Bible lesson, Luther came to these words in the book of Romans: "I am not ashamed of the gospel, because it is the power of God that brings salvation to everyone who believes: first to the Jew, then to the Gentile. For in the gospel the righteousness of God is revealed—a righteousness that is by faith from first to last" (1:16-17).

In these words, the apostle Paul, writing to the early church in Rome, was explaining the gospel, the good news that would eventually have a great impact on the whole Roman Empire. But why was this message so radical, so countercultural? And why do these verses stand as the theme of the entire book of Romans?

Let's begin by considering the phrase "the righteousness of God," which troubled Luther greatly. If God were not so righteous we would have a better chance of winning His favor, but it is His righteousness that stands as a barrier between us and Him. We can all identify with Luther's dilemma; we have all thought that if God were not so holy— if He were more like us—then we might be able to meet His requirements. But the Bible and even our own conscience tell us that we are sinners and we can't reach the high standard of God's righteousness by our own efforts. If only there were a way for us to receive the righteousness of God!

Yet—and here is why the gospel is good news—Luther learned, as we must, that righteousness is not just an attribute of God. There is also a "righteousness of God" which is a gift given to those who believe on Christ. To put it plainly, in Christ, God meets His own requirements for us. So although we have no righteousness of our own that God will accept, God rescues us by giving us His own righteousness as a free gift. In other words, God demands righteousness and holiness, and through the death and resurrection of Christ, *God supplies the righteousness that He demands*! And when it is time for us to die, we will be welcomed into heaven as if we were Jesus because we are saved solely on the perfections of His merit and grace.

And who benefits from this free gift? It is given to "everyone who believes." Paul made it clear that it is not one's ethnicity or religious upbringing that determines one's destiny; he said this message is "first to the Jew, then to the Gentile" (that is, it's for Jews and non-Jews). Paul said this message is received "by faith from first to last." To believe means that we acknowledge our own sinfulness and inability to save ourselves and thus we place our faith in Christ. No longer do we look to our own goodness to save us; rather, we accept the goodness of Christ, believing that He will do for us what we can't.

There are some who have defined the term *justification* as meaning "just as if I'd never sinned." But that is only half the story. It's not just that our slates are clean, wonderful though that is. It also means that God looks at us as if we have lived lives of perfect obedience. He sees us as being loving, submissive, pure. He sees us as having done everything Christ has done.

Many years ago I (Erwin) conducted a funeral for a man named Roger, who, as a homosexual, lived a life of obsessive immorality. Thankfully, he came to saving faith in Christ before his death from AIDS.

In his final days it would have been easy for Roger to focus on his past behavior, the guilt and regret of his past. But he didn't. He focused on his acceptance in Christ, that gift of perfect righteousness which would give him the assurance that he would be welcomed into heaven. I'm convinced that at death he entered heaven as perfect as God.

Imagine a book entitled *The Life and Times of Jesus Christ*. It speaks of all the perfections of Christ, the works that He did, the holy obedience, the purity, and the right motives. It is a beautiful book indeed.

Then imagine another book, this one entitled *The Life and Times of Roger*. It mentions all his sins—the immorality, the broken promises, and the betrayal of friends. It includes mention of sinful thoughts, mixed motives, and acts of disobedience.

Finally, imagine that Christ removes the covers from both books. Then He takes the pages of His own book and slips them between the covers of Roger's book. We pick up the book to examine it. The title reads *The Life and Times of Roger*. Yet as we begin to turn the pages, we find no sins mentioned. All we see is a long list of perfections—obedience, moral purity, and perfect love. The book is so beautiful that even God adores it.

The exchange described here is known as *justification*. In this way, God credits the loveliness of Christ to all of us who are woefully imperfect. Of course we have to be perfect to enter into heaven, and thanks to Christ, we are!

Once we have received the benefits of the gospel we will spend the rest of our lives loving and serving God. Imagine, if you will, a servant who works in a king's estate, but consistently criticizes the king, steals, tells lies, and refuses to obey the king's orders. This king has an obedient son whom he dearly loves. Then imagine the king saying to his beloved son, "I have chosen to love that wicked servant as much as I love you. But in order for him to be reconciled to me, you will have to die on his behalf, and pay the demands of justice for his sin." Upon the wicked servant understanding and accepting what the king has done for him, he obviously would love and serve that king to the best of his ability for the rest of his life. And this is exactly what God the Father did when He sent His Son, Jesus, to die on the cross.

As we saw earlier, justification is sometimes defined as "just as if I'd never sinned." That is true, but there's more to it than that. It also means "just as if I had the same righteousness as God," and thanks to Jesus, we do! No wonder Paul said that when we are justified we have "peace with God."

With such confidence, we have no reason to fear even death itself.

Taking God's Word to Heart

1. If the qualification for entrance into heaven is perfection, where do all of us stand in that regard? Can any human being ever qualify on the basis of his or her own merits?

2. Read Romans 1:16-17. Is it possible for us to be as perfect as God? If so, how?

3. Explain the gift of righteousness given to those who believe on Christ.

4. What does it mean to believe?

5. What is justification? What does God do? What must we do?

LOSS

*Job 1:21—Naked I came from my mother's womb,
and naked I will depart. The Lord gave and the Lord
has taken away; may the name of the Lord be praised.*

*Job 13:15—Though he slay me, yet will I hope in
him; I will surely defend my ways to his face.*

Job's day began uneventfully, but by nightfall he had lost his ten children. With ten fresh graves on a hilltop, he had to contemplate the anguish of the incredible loss to him and his wife. She evidently stood firm in her faith until Job was personally attacked with boils; at that point she suggested that her husband curse God and die (Job 2:9). But Job would not give up his integrity; his faith, though frayed, remained intact.

When you suffer loss you need friends who do not condemn you, but weep with you in your sorrow. You want others to help you process your grief. You do not want to hear a sermon about God's care, although it is the truths about His care that will sustain you in the days ahead. But what you really want—indeed, need—are people who will listen and in some measure share your grief. We always need friends, and at no time do we need them more than when we suffer unexpected loss.

Job was not blessed with these kinds of friends. His companions judged him, blaming him for his predicament. They believed that there was a tight connection between blessing and obedience. They concluded that he was at fault for all the tragedies that had come upon him.

In the end, Job learned that even when friends fail us, and even when we cannot make sense of what happened, God is still there, giving grace and showing mercy. And there are powerful lessons we can learn when sorrow overwhelms us.

For example, Job learned, as we all must, that every trial is a test to see how much God means to us. Is He worthy of worship apart from the blessings He gives us? Or do we serve God only because it is profitable for us to do so?

Let's revisit Satan's reply to God: "Does Job fear God for nothing?... Have you not put a hedge around him...?" (Job 1:9-10). In other words, the devil was telling God, "You are bribing Job for his worship and allegiance. He is serving You because of the blessings You have given him. Anyone would serve You if You gave them a fine family and wealth!" Job, Satan said, was serving God for the perks he got in return.

We face the same challenge almost every day. Do we serve God only when He gives us blessings? Is God good only when life goes our way? Or is God good even when our children are killed in a windstorm or murdered by an intruder? Must we be bribed into our commitment? How we respond to trials will answer those questions.

We learn from Job that when God wishes to test one of His servants, nothing is untouchable! We are startled to discover that Satan was given the power to have Job's ten children killed—ten lives with the potential of enjoyment and blessing! And because God wanted to try Job, if we may put it indelicately, these children were expendable.

God does not have to give us marriage partners, healthy families, fine homes, and happy times. He has the right to give us children and to take them; to keep us from sickness and to let us suffer. When He wants to test the depth of our allegiance, He can take that which is closest to our hearts.

We also learn that events on earth must be interpreted in light of events in heaven. Think this through: Job didn't know that God and the devil had a dialogue about him! He was not privy to the challenge that Satan laid before God somewhere in the heavenlies. If Job had known he was being watched by angels, demons, and God—if he had known he was a test case—he probably would have endured the trial much more easily.

Perhaps God and the devil have had a dialogue about you or us recently. You or we might be chosen for an unexpected test that will reverse our fortunes. Yes, we are being watched in the heavenlies. And whether we pass the test or fail it is more important in heaven than it is on earth.

Finally, Job reminds us that it is possible to worship God in the midst of unanswered questions. He did not have any warning for this trial; he received no revelation regarding its purposes. After hearing all the bad news, he received no memo providing a rationale for what happened. Nor did he receive assurance that all this would end with greater blessing. The tragedy struck suddenly, with no warning and no opportunity for recourse.

As Job's heart pounded with grief, he fell on his face and worshiped. He did not curse God, nor did he demand an explanation. He accepted God's right to give and to take.

We all know of tragic deaths surrounded by unanswered questions. A couple whose son's death was ruled a suicide is convinced he was actually murdered. Another couple whose child was found dead in a ditch has no explanation for what happened.

At a conference a man said, "My son committed suicide…if he is not in heaven, I don't want to go there myself. I would rather be in hell." Perhaps his son is in heaven; we trust it is so. Meanwhile this distraught father must learn to worship God without knowing his child's fate. He must believe that whatever God does, He indeed has the right to do. As we like to say, we as Christians live by promises, not explanations.

We all will have to wait until we get to heaven to find out the whys and the wherefores. And in the meantime, we can be grateful for those who have not abandoned their faith in spite of great suffering even as God's purposes remain hidden.

I walked a mile with Pleasure;
She chatted all the way;
But left me none the wiser
For all she had to say.
I walked a mile with Sorrow;
And ne'er a word said she;
But, oh! The things I learned from her,
When Sorrow walked with me.

—ROBERT BROWNING HAMILTON

God is with us in our successes and losses. We must trust Him at all times, no matter what happens.

Taking God's Word to Heart

1. One lesson Job learned was that every trial is a test to see how much God means to us. Some trials are more difficult than others. In the midst of a trial, were you ever tempted to lose faith in God? What encouraged you to continue and endure the test?

2. Do you at times find your service to God conditional? Are we inclined to serve Him only when He blesses us? How do you respond to trials when no blessings are in sight?

3. Share a time when your allegiance to God was severely tested. What promises from Scripture did you embrace?

4. When it comes to difficult circumstances surrounded by unanswered questions, are you willing to simply trust God and learn the whys and wherefores later? What is the benefit of such trust?

5. We know from Job's account that God can do whatever He chooses for the sake of His glory. As Scripture says, Job lost his ten children. Here is a difficult question: How do you think you would have responded had you been Job?

LOVE

1 Corinthians 13:1-3—*If I speak in the tongues of men or of angels, but do not have love, I am only a resounding gong or a clanging cymbal. If I have the gift of prophecy and can fathom all mysteries and all knowledge, and if I have a faith that can move mountains, but do not have love, I am nothing. If I give all I possess to the poor and give over my body to hardship that I may boast, but do not have love, I gain nothing.*

John 3:16—*God so loved the world that he gave his one and only Son, that whoever believes in him shall not perish but have eternal life.*

In the New Testament we are commanded to speak the *truth* in *love* (Ephesians 4:15), but maintaining this balance is difficult. Truth people often come up short on love; love people often sacrifice truth. We are frequently tempted to lean toward one side or the other.

Paul has the harshest words for the person who prides himself on his works and abilities but lacks love. He says that such a person is "only a resounding gong or a clanging cymbal." Indeed, if you had faith to remove mountains but did not have love, you are nothing! For us, this means that if we teach a Sunday school class, or we're generous in our giving, or we do volunteer work at a homeless shelter, yet we do not have love, we have missed the point of our existence.

This kind of love is remarkable: It is patient and kind; it is able to persevere under difficult circumstances. Although faith will give way to sight and hope will disappear in the presence of reality, love will endure. It is an eternal virtue. Love enables us to treat others the way we would want to be treated; it does not hold grudges nor does it seek advantage for itself; this love always exalts the needs of others above one's own needs. It protects the reputation of others.

Love is greatly misunderstood in our day. Often it is confused either with sentimentality or identified with the sexual relationship. Often we hear people say, "We're not married, but we love each other so much it's all right for us to live together." Or people show love only as long as it is convenient to do so. They profess love while living a selfish lifestyle that masquerades as a caring relationship.

Human love is a wonderful experience, both when we are the recipient of its benefits and when we extend it to others. But human love, by itself, is unable to endure when times become difficult. Human love can even hold a difficult marriage together, but more often than not, it reaches its breaking point quite quickly.

Divine love, which Paul had in mind when he wrote 1 Corinthians 13, is not merely human emotion. Rather, it is based on an intimate relationship with God. Human love is based on the one who is loved; human love says, "I love you because of what you do for me. I love you because you are loveable; I love you because you fulfill my life." This kind of love is often based on the appearance ("you are beautiful; therefore I love you"), or on an appealing personality ("you are engaging, funny, and great to be around"), and therefore this love is subject to change. It's easy to love those who are physically attractive or those with a magnetic personality. But this love can easily wither when hard times come.

Divine love is based on the lover: Divine love says, "I can still love you even if you change; I can still love you even when you disappoint me." Just as Jesus was willing to die for us when we were His enemies, so our love should be willing to transcend the disappointments that can enter into a relationship.

This love is generated within us by the Holy Spirit; it is the natural outworking of the Spirit's power in the life of a person who has chosen to die to self-interest and submit to God's leadership in his or her life. The fruit of the Holy Spirit is, first of all, love, which is birthed in our hearts (see Galatians 5:22).

This love should be evident in our marriages, in our family relationships, and of course, to the world around us. The people of the world can out-finance us, they can outnumber us, and they can out-entertain us, but let it never be said that they can out-love us.

Hymn writer Charles Weigle was speaking at a Bible conference in Pasadena, California, and when he arrived at the meeting on Sunday evening, a friend asked, "Did you enjoy the rose garden this afternoon?" Weigle was a bit surprised because he had told no one what he had been doing before coming to the service. "You brought the fragrance of the roses with you," his friend said.

And so it is: We are called to bring the loving fragrance of Christ to a world that is in desperate need of a message of help and hope. And when we are in the presence of others, they should know that we love because we have been loved.

Divine love should be worn as a badge by all followers of Jesus Christ.

Taking God's Word to Heart

1. What are the characteristics of divine love as described in 1 Corinthians 13? Contrast this kind of love with the shallow counterparts we find in the world.

2. Ephesians 4:15 commands us to speak "the truth in love." What does that lead to?

3. What is the enduring value of divine love? Why is it enduring?

4. Upon what is human love based? Upon what is divine love based?

5. Where does divine love come from? In what ways should this love be evident in lives?

PEACE

John 14:27—*Peace I leave with you; my peace I give
you. I do not give to you as the world gives. Do not
let your hearts be troubled and do not be afraid.*

Philippians 4:7—*The peace of God, which
transcends all understanding, will guard your
hearts and your minds in Christ Jesus.*

Everyone seeks for peace. The Sunday school teacher wants peace,
the drug dealer wants peace, and the alcoholic wants peace. We all
seek peace. The question is, Where can we find it?

There are inner thieves that come to steal our peace: guilt, self-
loathing, fear, anger, and worry, to name a few. Also, there are thieves
that come from outside of us: the people we live with, the colleagues
we work with, our pressing finances, our deteriorating health. All of
these, and more, can rob us of peace.

Peace does not mean the absence of grief and tears. Jesus, though at
peace with Himself and His Father, struggled through the horrors of
Gethsemane and the cross. Peace means having a deep-seated sense of
stability, a sense of being guided by God; it is something like hope, but
it is more immediate. Peace is something we can experience right now,
no matter what our circumstance.

To discover more about this peace, let's consider these five words
from the lips of Jesus: "My peace I give you."

Note the word "my." We are talking about the peace that belongs to
Jesus. It originates with Him and becomes ours because we belong to

Him. It's a three-dimensional kind of peace. First, we have peace with God: "Since we have been justified through faith, we have peace with God through our Lord Jesus Christ" (Romans 5:1). Sin made God our enemy. Sin separated us from God's presence. When Jesus came, He reconciled us to God by paying our debt and giving us peace. And this, incidentally, is the answer to those inner thieves of peace that want to ruin us. Guilt, discouragement, regret, the crushing feeling of self-condemnation (which is often brought about by my sin and the devil) are removed by Christ making peace between us and God. To experience forgiveness with God is to possess peace.

There is a second dimension, and that is peace with one another. Paul taught that by bringing peace, Jesus has made both Jew and Gentile one (Ephesians 2:14-16). The animosity between Jews and Gentiles was like the antagonism between the Arabs and the Jews of today. But in Jesus, these groups are reconciled. And if Paul were writing to the American church, he would say, "He has made us all one, blacks and whites, Asians and Latinos, and everyone else." Because when we are at peace with God, we can be at peace with others. And if we aren't, we need to be reconciled; we need to ask one another's forgiveness; we need to humble ourselves.

There is a third dimension, and that is personal. Christ says, "I can give you peace within your heart." I've heard some people described as a cauldron, as if they have a civil war going on inside of them. Perhaps as you read this, you would admit you are filled with emptiness and unrest. Jesus can bring rest to your soul. Reconciled to God and others, you can have personal peace.

The second word we ought to note is "give." This peace is a gift. Because it is a gift, it isn't tied to circumstances. It is a gift that is inserted in the midst of our circumstances, independent of how bad things may be. In every situation, Jesus can give us the gift of His peace. It is an unearned gift. We can know this peace even if our circumstances remain unchanged.

Finally, Jesus said He will give this peace to "you." Jesus knows your past history. He knows what you're going through, and He knows what your tomorrows hold. He knows all the contingencies, all the possibilities; He sees your coming promotions and demotions. He already knows when and where you will die and what will be said at your funeral. And He can bring peace to you no matter where you are along the continuum of life.

Jesus made this promise shortly before He was to experience the treachery of Judas, the betrayal of Peter, and the horrors of Gethsemane and the cross. Satan wanted to disrupt Jesus' peace, but Jesus made it clear the prince of this world had no hold on Him.

How can this peace be ours? Isaiah wrote, "You will keep in perfect peace those whose minds are steadfast, because they trust in you" (26:3). We can keep our minds steadfast by memorizing Scripture passages, singing hymns, and meeting with the people of God. Focusing on God's promises does not happen automatically; it is a struggle, but it yields peaceable results. Yes, Jesus really does give His peace to those who focus on Him alone rather than their circumstances, difficulties, pain, and heartache.

Somewhere we came across this bit of doggerel:

> All the water in the world
> However hard it tried,
> Could never, never sink a ship
> Unless it got inside.
> All the evil in the world,
> the wickedness and sin,
> Can never sink your soul's fair craft
> Unless you let it in.

When Arthur Mursell, a minister, visited Waterloo, where the British defeated the French emperor Napoleon Bonaparte, he saw a huge bronze lion that had been made from the guns that the British captured in that great battle. This lion snarls with his mouth open and his teeth protruding as he overlooks the battlefield. Mursell said he noticed that a bird had built a nest in the lion's mouth, with twigs sticking out from among the lion's teeth. And there were birds freely chirping in the lion's mouth.[12]

Thanks to Jesus, we too can be at peace—even when we are in the lion's mouth.

Taking God's Word to Heart

1. In John 14:27, Jesus speaks of a peace that He can give. How do we as believers receive it?

2. One dimension of peace is the peace we have as individuals with God. What does Romans 5:1 tell us about this peace? Name some "inner thieves" we must guard against that can rob us of this peace.

3. How does our peace with God relate to our peace with others? How does it relate to the inner peace within our hearts? What role does forgiveness play with our experiencing peace?

4. The peace God gives is a supernatural peace that is able to help us in every circumstance, no matter how difficult. Share about times when you have experienced God's peace in the midst of difficulty.

5. What promise do we find in Isaiah 26:3? What activities can help us remain steadfast and strengthen our faith during difficult times? What Scripture passages do you embrace for strength?

PRAYER

Mark 1:35—*Very early in the morning, while
it was still dark, Jesus got up, left the house and
went off to a solitary place, where he prayed.*

Ephesians 6:18—*Pray in the Spirit in all occasions with
all kinds of prayers and requests. With this in mind, be
alert and always keep on praying for all the Lord's people.*

When I (Erwin) asked Jim Cymbala, of the Brooklyn Tabernacle in New York, why people stood outside the door of his church on a Tuesday evening waiting for the doors to open so they would be among the first to find a seat for the weekly prayer meeting, he answered simply, "Your church would also be filled every week for prayer meeting if the people believed that God answered prayer…and that things would be different after they prayed."

How simple but true! Every church would be filled for prayer meeting if people actually believed that God answered prayer and that prayer changes circumstances. However, truth be told, some people who have seen their prayers left unanswered have become cynical and think that prayer has no personal benefits. And sadly, many churches no longer take time to have prayer meetings. Moreover, many believers spend only a few minutes in prayer each day, usually asking God for the same routine requests.

How can we break such disinterest or routine? And how can we restore prayer to its proper place in our lives? First, we have to grapple with the widespread assumption that the sovereignty of God is an impediment to prayer. The argument goes like this: Because God has a certain plan that He intends to carry out, and because He has limitless power to do so, how can my prayer possibly affect His will? Conclusion: "Whatever will be will be."

Interestingly, Jesus taught that God's sovereignty was not a hindrance to prayer, but rather a *basis* for prayer. He told the disciples that they should not become repetitious like the heathen, who thought they would be heard because of their many words. Then Jesus taught the disciples how to pray by giving what is commonly known as the Lord's Prayer (read Matthew 6:5-14). Note that the fact our heavenly Father has prior knowledge of all events should not discourage us from praying, but give us confidence as we pray!

Don't let the puzzle of God's sovereignty and what is commonly called our free will be a hindrance to your prayers. In fact, these things should *motivate* us to ask great things of God.

Second, it is clear from Scripture that God wants us to move beyond our litany of routine requests to develop a relationship with Him. If we see the first purpose of prayer as getting our petitions answered, we might end up like a whiny child whose attitude toward his father depends entirely on whether he gets what he wants when he wants it. We will think that one day God is kind because He answers a prayer, and the next day He is indifferent because we don't get what we want. Given that focus, no wonder prayer meetings don't have better attendance!

Now, it is true that God can do whatever He wants whether we pray or not. So it stands to reason that the first purpose of prayer is *not* to get our requests answered, as such. The reason God permits us to experience so many needs is that they are what nudges us into His presence. And once we are there, our focus shifts and we realize we need God's presence more than we need the answers we seek. If we draw near to God because we enjoy His companionship, we will discover that the first purpose of prayer will always be achieved whether or not we get the answer we want.

This kind of praying is driven by praise and thanksgiving; it is a kind of prayer that submits to God and finds delight in being in His presence. This changes prayer from being a boring or seemingly irrelevant experience and turns it into a time of intimate fellowship with our heavenly Father. This kind of praying seeks the Lord Himself, not just His answers to our lists of requests.

Jesus often spent whole nights in prayer and yet this did not spare Him the trauma of Gethsemane and the painful humiliation of the cross. It is clear that for Him, fellowship with the Father was His highest priority. He knew that if He was intimately connected with His Father, He could endure whatever lay ahead.

Ironically, we need fellowship with God more than we need funds to pay our bills or to have our health restored. Please don't think that we are minimizing these necessities of life; we are only saying that lying at the heart of these issues is our relationship with God. Only when we are comfortable in His presence will we be able to accept life as it comes to us. God's first priority is not to change our circumstances, but to change us.

Third, we must realize that once God has been restored to His rightful place in our prayer life, praying in His will becomes easier and doable. Now we are able to approach Him with an attitude of submission; we can even "hear His voice" not in words to be sure, but deep within there is a peace that profoundly accepts whatever God gives us. And, no matter what happens, we know God has permitted it and is with us.

When the apostle Paul said we should "pray in the Spirit" (Ephesians 6:18), he was referring to a connection with God that not only acknowledges His sovereignty but also recognizes that what God does *in* us is often more important than what God does *through* us, or what He does outside of us.

It is from this kind of relationship that petitions flow with a right attitude from our hearts to God. Only on the strength of the intimacy of our relationship with God can we give our requests to Him and be at peace. Then our hearts are guarded because our relationship with God remains firm regardless of the outcome of our prayer requests.

Yes, we might draw more people to a prayer meeting if we saw more answers to prayer. But we would also increase our numbers if we all had the faith to believe that God is actively at work whether we get exactly what we ask for or not. To accept the invitation to meet with God individually or collectively is our highest privilege. When we move from requests to relationship, we enter into the heart of what God had in mind when we were told to pray continuously without fainting.

Remember, desperation leads us to prayer...and prayer leads us to the heart of God.

Taking God's Word to Heart

1. How important is prayer to your life of faith? How much time do you spend seeking God in prayer?

2. Read again the comments about God's sovereignty. How does God's control of all things relate to our prayer life? How is it a basis for our prayers?

3. What should be our first purpose in prayer? What should be our focus during prayer?

4. What was Jesus' approach to prayer as we see it in the Gospels? What characterized His prayers? What were His priorities?

5. Why is the quality of our relationship with God so important to our prayer life? As we seek God in prayer, what happens when we change our focus from requests to relationship?

PURITY

Proverbs 4:23—*Above all else, guard your heart, for everything you do flows from it.*

Matthew 5:8—*Blessed are the pure in heart, for they will see God.*

Your first and highest duty is the guarding of your soul.

John Bunyan, in his famous book *The Holy War,* said that for strength our souls might be called a castle; for pleasantness they might be called a paradise; and for largeness, they might be called a palace. "This palace the King intends but for Himself alone, and not another with Him, and He commits the keeping of that palace day and night to the men of the town." Yes, we are asked by God to keep the palace—our hearts and minds—for the King alone. This inner realm, known intimately only to us and not another human, is more important than our bodies could ever be.

Unfortunately, ever since the fall of man, invaders have taken over the soul: pride, jealousy, greed, lust, anger, self-aggrandizement; these and more like them have done their dastardly work. These evils take up residence within us, carefully hidden from the prying eyes of men but not the penetrating eyes of God. To get our stubborn, sin-loving hearts to bow down to the sovereignty of the King is always our most urgent task.

First, we must ask God to search our hearts and help us uncover what is there. This first but necessary step is difficult for the simple reason that we won't like what we find. We are naturally prone to flee from our true selves; we are quick to justify ourselves, to compare ourselves favorably with others, and to make a myriad of excuses. Here honesty must reign, for if we come to God with our minds made up about ourselves and with a sheaf of excuses for our sins, these will grow within us like weeds in an unattended garden.

Second, we must take the time to ask God to help us identify the doors that these invaders use to occupy our souls. In what environment do they flourish, and what changes should we make to minimize their entry? We must be willing to part with friends, books, television shows, movies, and relationships that are stimuli that exacerbate the sins we have come to love and tolerate. We must give Christ the key to every door of our heart, including the closets where especially loved sins are safely stored for future use. Desperation to be free from these sins that invade our lives is always necessary. This is no time for a halfhearted confession made with the full intention of repeating the sin when conditions are favorable.

We must ask God to cleanse our souls, to purify our hearts so that the sins we have patiently tolerated are expelled. "If we confess our sins, he is faithful and just and will forgive us our sins and purify us from all unrighteousness" (1 John 1:9).

We must give constant attention to our hearts because the baser appetites of the soul will repeatedly seek to regain entry into our lives. If we naively do not anticipate their return, they will overwhelm us with their promises to satisfy our deepest needs. The cleansed soul must now dedicate itself to being filled with those thoughts that give prominence to the King who owns the castle, to use Bunyan's terminology. There can be no substitute for the memorization of Scripture, fellowship with other believers, and such other disciplines of the Christian faith.

Jesus promised that the pure in heart will see God. The soul that finds delight in God is led into the satisfaction of fellowship with the Most High. This fellowship must be guarded at all costs.

Every hour spent guarding our hearts is an hour that will please the Lord and make us more like Him.

Taking God's Word to Heart

1. What are some of the struggles we face as we strive to maintain our purity and guard our souls?

2. Asking God to search our hearts is a first step toward purity. Why is this often a painful exercise?

3. If we honestly seek purity, we must be honest and ruthless with ourselves, willing to rid our hearts and minds of the sins and activities that rob us of purity. What kinds of steps do we need to take to make that happen?

4. Read 1 John 1:9. Why is it essential to stand guard against sins that attempt to reenter our hearts and minds?

5. One way to guard our souls is to read God's Word. In this way, we fill our minds and hearts with God's thoughts. Discuss additional steps and activities that can help us guard our souls.

REDEMPTION

1 Peter 1:18-19—*You know that it was not with
perishable things such as silver or gold that you were
redeemed from the empty way of life handed down
to you from your ancestors, but with the precious
blood of Christ, a lamb without blemish or defect.*

The meaning of the word *redemption* would have been much clearer to the apostle Peter's readers than it is to us today. Back in his time, there were millions of slaves who could have been redeemed from slavery if someone had been willing to pay the stipulated price to win their freedom. Then, if they had been redeemed, they could have not only have been brought out of the slave market, but they would also have been free to serve their new owner.

Just so, we are born into the slave market of sin, and as we grow up we prove our sinfulness by personally sinning, and we compound our guilt by justifying our sin to ourselves and to others. We cannot pay our own purchase price of redemption, for, spiritually speaking, we are bankrupt, hopelessly indebted to God.

Thankfully, Jesus came to do what we could not. Listen to His own job description: "The Son of Man did not come to be served, but to serve, and to give his life as a ransom for many" (Mark 10:45). He paid a price that we could not, and He did it to set us free from our slavery to sin and Satan.

Redemption, then, is the means by which salvation is achieved—namely, by the payment of a ransom. To redeem is to "buy out of a marketplace." God's deliverance of His people from Egypt is spoken of as redemption; thus God is called Israel's Redeemer. The Israelites were slaves in Egypt, and only by a demonstration of God's personal and powerful intervention could they be freed.

The best example of redemption is found in Exodus 12, where God told Moses to instruct each Israelite household to kill a lamb without any blemish and sprinkle its blood on the doorposts of the house, thus averting the judgment of the angel of death. The lamb died in the place of the household's firstborn son, hence the son was "redeemed" from judgment by the substitute lamb. Just so, we are redeemed from eternal death by our substitute, Jesus Christ, who died in our place so that we could be acquitted of our sin and receive God's righteousness.

In the above passage Peter stresses two facts: First, he details our need to be bought out of the slavery of sin, which he describes as an "empty way of life" handed down from our forefathers. Our predicament is that we cannot redeem ourselves because we do not have a perfect payment that God would accept.

Second, Peter stresses the awesome nature of the payment made for us. Silver and gold are usually thought to be among the safest investments for preserving our money; witness how their value escalates at a time of crisis. Peter calls even these valued assets "perishable things" in contrast to the incomparable value of "the precious blood of Christ." If the value of an item is dependent on the price paid for it, then we are indeed valuable, for we have been bought at high cost.

To whom was the purchase price paid? Even though we were held captive by the devil before our conversion, the purchase price was not paid to him, but to God. Of course all things already belong to God, but the price Jesus paid was perfectly designed to satisfy God's holy anger against sin; He was a perfect sacrifice that our heavenly Father accepted on our behalf.

What are the implications of our redemption? The most obvious is that we now belong to God and are no longer subject to our former masters—namely sin and the devil. In the words of Paul, "He has rescued us from the dominion of darkness and brought us into the kingdom of the Son he loves, in whom we have redemption, the forgiveness of sins" (Colossians 1:13-14). Thanks to Jesus, who paid the ransom, we have now officially switched owners, and both our identities and destinies have been forever changed. We can act on what God has done for us by believing that we have indeed been set free from the horrid curse of sin and its fearful penalty.

Peter stated that the doctrine of redemption is the basis for our moral and spiritual purity. "Now that you have purified yourselves by obeying the truth so that you have sincere love for each other, love one another deeply, from the heart" (1 Peter 1:22). Now that a new owner has bought us, we have an obligation to willingly become His follower and pursue His plans for us. Redemption lies at the heart of a radical life-change in both our values and aspirations.

Scholar Everett F. Harrison commented, "No word in the Christian vocabulary deserves to be held more precious than Redeemer, for even more than Savior it reminds the child of God that his salvation has been purchased at great and personal cost, for the Lord has given himself for our sins in order to deliver us from them."[13]

Redemption means that someone loved us enough to buy our freedom. To Him we should gladly give our deepest loyalty and praise.

No wonder we often sing as Fanny J. Crosby did:

> Redeemed how I love to proclaim it!
> Redeemed by the blood of the Lamb;
> Redeemed thro' His infinite mercy,
> His child, and forever, I am.[14]

Taking God's Word to Heart

1. In Bible times, the concept of redemption had a cultural context. What did redemption mean to Peter's readers?

2. As it applies to our release from slavery to sin, explain the

biblical doctrine of redemption. What does Mark 10:45 tell us about the price paid to set us free from our obligations to sin and Satan?

3. Read 1 Peter 1:18-19. What two key facts does Peter raise about our need to be bought out from the slavery of sin?

4. What are the implications of our redemption? (See Colossians 1:13-14.)

5. Based on our redemption from sin, what obligations are we to fulfill?

RENEWING THE MIND

Romans 12:1-2—*I urge you, brothers and sisters, in view of God's mercy, to offer your bodies as a living sacrifice, holy and pleasing to God—this is your true and proper worship. Do not conform to the pattern of this world, but be transformed by the renewing of your mind. Then you will be able to test and approve what God's will is—his good, pleasing and perfect will.*

2 Corinthians 10:5—*We demolish arguments and every pretension that sets itself up against the knowledge of God, and we take captive every thought to make it obedient to Christ.*

Have you given your anxiety to God only to find an hour later that the weight of your concern is back on your shoulders? Do you ask God to help you control your temper, but still blow your top? Have you prayed against lust, and even reckoned yourself dead to sinful impulses, only to find yourself struggling again with pornography?

Jesus told a story that illustrates the most important single principle in breaking a sinful habit. When a man was inhabited by an evil spirit, and then the demon was expelled, the evil spirit then passed through waterless places, seeking rest. Finding none, it decided to return to the man. To its satisfaction, the demon saw that its original living space was unoccupied. It then found seven other spirits even more evil than itself to go and live there with it. Sadly, the man, who just a short time earlier had been dancing with joy, was now worse off than he had been before (Luke 11:24-26).

Why did this man fail in his quest for freedom? He didn't understand the principle of replacement. None of us can overcome evil by simply renouncing it. Rather, we must substitute that which was evil and replace it with that which is good. Sinful habits cannot be broken without replacing them with righteous ones. Try this simple experiment: Think of the number eight. Have you visualized it? If yes, then use your willpower to stop thinking about the number eight right now.

Were you able to do it? Of course not. Can you, by sheer willpower, stop thinking about the number eight? By no means. Trying to push it out of your mind actually causes you to focus your attention on it.

Although we can't stop thinking about that number by sheer resistance, we can push it out of our minds quite easily. Here's how: Think about a few bits of information you remember about your mother while growing up. Reminisce about your place in the family, whether you are still connected with them or disconnected. Concentrate on this new information, and you'll stop thinking of the number eight.

You can handle sinful thought patterns in the same way. Fear, lust, covetousness, anger—all of these can be pushed out of your mind by turning your thoughts to the Scriptures. Freedom comes by filling your mind with God's thoughts.

We know a young man whose wife died of cancer. She suffered intensely during the last weeks of her life. Yet she and her husband were able to accept this tragedy without bitterness or the slightest trace of self-pity. We asked him, "Why were you and your wife able to accept this so well? Weren't you ever resentful and angry at God through this ordeal?" His reply: "Yes, we had moments like that. But when they came, I read the Scriptures to my wife. Then we bought the whole New Testament on CD, and we played it in our house, hour after hour." That was the secret—expelling angry and anxious thoughts by filling the mind with the Word of God.

What is the best way to take air out of a bottle? Possibly someone could suggest that we build an elaborate vacuum pump to suck out the air. But there is a simpler solution. If we fill the bottle with water, the air is forced to leave.

To diffuse the power of sin, you need to have your negative thought patterns replaced by thoughts from the Word of God. Every temptation, vice, or sinister motive comes to you by your thoughts; these must be brought under the control of the Holy Spirit. The difference between worldliness and godliness is a renewed mind. This old adage puts it straight: You aren't what you think you are; but what you *think*, you are!

Let us suggest that you get started right now:

Begin by identifying the alien thoughts you want replaced. You must name the fantasies, imaginations, and attitudes that you want to be rid of. To say, "I want to be a better Christian" or "I want to be a happier person" will not do. Generalities will not work here. Then find a Scripture passage that applies specifically to your particular temptation. You can do this with the help of a concordance, or you can find these passages through your own reading of God's Word.

Next, declaring war on your thought life means you must set aside time every morning to begin your offensive attack. We suggest 20 minutes as a minimum. Meditation upon and memorization of the Scriptures requires effort; nothing worth having can be achieved without exertion. And along with this discipline comes the need to draw near to God in faith and grow in your love for Him and trust in Him.

During the day, learn to obey the first promptings of the Holy Spirit. If you are tempted to enjoy a sensual fantasy, deal with those thoughts immediately. Each of us knows when we let our minds skip across that invisible line into forbidden territory. The moment we do so, we sense we are violating the purity that the Holy Spirit desires. That is the moment to say, "In the name of Jesus, I reject these thoughts." And then quote the passages of Scripture you have learned for that temptation. Over time, your sensitivity to the Holy Spirit's conviction of your heart will continue to grow.

Use your temptation as an alarm system—as a signal that it's time for you to give praise to God. If, for example, you fear cancer (since one out of four people in the United States will get some form of cancer, your fears may have a statistical basis), use that fear as an opportunity to give glory to God. Quote Romans 8:35-39 or read Psalms 103, 144, or 145. Then thank God for all the blessings you have in Christ. Thank Him for forgiveness, for His sovereignty, power, and love. In this way, your stumbling block will be changed into a stepping stone. You'll be praising rather than pouting.

How long does it take for the mind to be renewed? That depends. Some Christians who apply these principles recognize a noticeable difference within a week. Others who are steeped in decades of sin may need months before they can say, "I am free!" And, of course, no one reaches perfection. The more we meditate on the Word, the more clearly we see new areas of our lives that need change. Subtle motives often surface only after long exposure to the light of God's Word.

So start now—replace your sinful thoughts with thoughts from God's Word. A renewed mind is the doorway to a renewed life.

Taking God's Word to Heart

1. Read again Jesus' story about the man inhabited by a demon. What was the point of the story?

2. Explain the principle of replacement. How does it apply to the breaking of sinful habits?

3. How does reading God's Word diffuse the power of sin? How are we aided by the Holy Spirit in these matters?

4. Consider the statement, "The difference between godliness and worldliness is a renewed mind." How important is it for us to maintain a daily intake of truth from God's Word? Why can Scripture memorization serve as an effective method of storing God's thoughts in your mind?

5. In this chapter is a four-step approach for renewing one's mind. Review these steps. Are you prepared to engage these steps and invest the effort and discipline necessary to renew your mind?

REWARDS

*1 Corinthians 3:13-15—Their work will be shown
for what it is, because the Day will bring it to light. It
will be revealed with fire, and the fire will test the
quality of each person's work. If what has been built
survives, the builder will receive a reward. If it is burned
up, the builder will suffer loss but yet will be saved—
even though only as one escaping through the flames.*

*2 Corinthians 5:10—We must all appear before
the judgment seat of Christ, so that each of us
may receive what is due us for the things done
while in the body, whether good or bad.*

He will wipe every tear from their eyes" (Revelations 21:4).
Have you ever wondered why there will be tears in heaven?
Possibly it is because we will realize that some of those whom we loved
the most will not spend eternity with us, but will be lost forever. Or, we
might find ourselves shedding tears of regret when we think back upon
how we squandered our lives despite the opportunities God gave us.
After all, even as believers we will give an account "for the things done
while in the body, whether good or bad."

Just imagine: We will all stand individually in the presence of Jesus,
who will thoroughly evaluate our lives to determine the rewards we will
receive. We're not suggesting we will see our sins, since they have been
forgiven by Christ and therefore will not be held against us. Neverthe-
less, our lives will be thoroughly reviewed. What if God were to take all

we have done (and not done) and turned these deeds and attitudes into either gold, silver, and precious stones, or into wood, hay, and stubble? Then when He puts a torch to the heap, the fire will "test the quality of each person's work" (1 Corinthians 3:13). In this way, our lives could be tested even without us seeing our sin.

We won't be judged for what we did prior to our conversion; in other words, we will not be judged for what we did since our "first birth," but what we have done since our "second birth." The apostle Paul evidently expected to do well at the judgment seat, even though he was a violent criminal before his conversion, throwing Christians into prison and supporting those who killed them. At the end of his life, Paul wrote, "I have fought the good fight, I have finished the race, I have kept the faith. Now there is in store for me the crown of righteousness, which the Lord, the righteous Judge, will award to me on that day—and not only to me, but also to all who have longed for his appearing" (2 Timothy 4:7-8).

Ponder the implications of this coming judgment.

First, every day is either a loss or a gain (or a mixture of both) as far as our future judgment is concerned. The great evangelist George Whitefield requested that these words be carved onto his gravestone: "I am content to wait till the day of judgment for the clearing up of my character. And after I am dead I desire no other epitaph than this, 'Here lies G.W. What sort of man he was the great day will discover.'" The anger of Whitefield's critics and the praise of his friends will not count; only what Jesus says and thinks will really matter. At issue will not be the size of our ministries or even the extent of our influence, but rather whether we lived wholeheartedly for God.

Second, if we are faithful, our reward will be to rule with Christ in the coming kingdom. Although it might well be that all Christians get to reign with Christ, the Bible makes such a privilege conditional: "If we endure, we will also reign with him" (2 Timothy 2:12). And if all Christians do reign with Him, as most Bible teachers believe, it is clear that those who are most faithful will be given more responsibilities in the life to come (Luke 19:11-27). Be assured that how you live on earth as a Christian has eternal implications.

Finally, it is possible that we can lose the approval of Christ. Not all Christians will hear Him say, "Well done, my good servant!" (verse 17). Our most pressing responsibility is to live passionately for Jesus Christ so that we will not be ashamed at His coming. Jesus is generous, and He is committed to rewarding us beyond our imagination.

There is a story, a legend that comes to us from India. A beggar saw a wealthy rajah come toward him, riding on his beautiful chariot. The beggar took advantage of the opportunity and stood by the side of the road holding out his bowl of rice, hoping for a handout. To his surprise, the rajah stopped, looked at him, and said, "Give me some of your rice!"

The beggar was angry—to think that this wealthy prince would expect his rice! Gingerly, he gave him one grain of rice.

"Beggar, give me more of your rice!"

In anger, the beggar gave him another grain of rice.

"More please!"

By now the beggar was seething with resentment. Once again he stingily gave the rajah another grain of rice, and then walked away. As the chariot went on its way, the beggar, in his fury, looked into his bowl. He noticed something glittering in the sunlight. It was a grain of gold, the size of a grain of rice. He looked more carefully and found just two more.

For every grain of rice he had given, he had gotten a grain of gold.

If we clutch our bowl of rice, we shall lose our reward. If we are faithful and give God each grain, He gives us gold in return.

And the gold God gives will survive the fire.

Taking God's Word to Heart

1. What goes through your mind as you consider the prospect of standing before Jesus and having your Christian service evaluated? Are you doing your best to serve Him in this life?

2. Every day is an opportunity to serve Jesus and impact your

future judgment. Might you discover other ways you can be of greater service to our Lord?

3. Read 2 Timothy 2:12 and Luke 19:11-27. How will faithful service on our part be rewarded in the coming kingdom?

4. It may well be that some Christians will find they have lost approval with Jesus due to their lack of faithfulness. With that possibility in view, what is our most pressing responsibility?

5. Consider the story about the generosity of a beggar. Perhaps we can only speculate about God's generosity when it will come to rewards. What are your thoughts about God's generosity in this life and what might take place in the next?

SATAN

James 4:7-10—*Submit yourselves, then, to God. Resist the devil, and he will flee from you. Come near to God and he will come near to you. Wash your hands, you sinners, and purify your hearts, you double-minded. Grieve, mourn and wail. Change your laughter to mourning and your joy to gloom. Humble yourselves before the Lord, and he will lift you up.*

1 Peter 5:8-9—*Be alert and of sober mind. Your enemy the devil prowls around like a roaring lion looking for someone to devour. Resist him, standing firm in the faith, because you know that the family of believers throughout the world is undergoing the same kind of sufferings.*

Satan is on the prowl, stalking and setting traps for God's people (and yes, for unbelievers too). He stays out of view, waiting for an unguarded moment. If we could know the extent of his knowledge of us, if we could understand his fiendish delight should we become a discredit to Christ, we would pore over the Scriptures to learn more about him and about the weaponry God has given us for the battle.

Satan himself is abhorrent to us. Knowing that, he comes to us using different disguises and different names. His goal is to get us to do something *he* wants us to do, all the while making us think that the idea is wholly ours.

Understandably, his chief point of attack is the human mind. He has varying degrees of access (depending on the amount of sin we tolerate) and uses his opportunities to the hilt. Since he is not a gentleman and plays only by his own rules, he influences our thoughts and feelings without a formal invitation. He is most pleased when his activity is completely hidden.

To alleviate any suspicion or fear, he gives his ideas familiar names that make us feel comfortable. Just as it would be foolish for us to think we could catch a mouse without a trap, so Satan knows that he must remain hidden. Yet behind the trap is the trapper; behind the lie is the liar. Even the wolf in *Little Red Riding Hood* was cunning enough to know that he could not say to the grandmother, "Let me in, for I am the wolf!" Instead he disguised his voice and whispered, "I'm Little Red Riding Hood!"

Satan's full-time occupation is making sin look good to us. Whatever the lure he employs, it is a highly intelligent spiritual being who plots our downfall. His intention is to cause us shame and to neutralize our effectiveness for Christ.

Satan also has tens of thousands of lesser spirits under his authority who have varying degrees of intelligence and power. They are highly organized and are forced to become his mercenaries, his servants who do his bidding. If they disobey, they are likely punished by their cruel leader.

Of course, there would still be addictions, violence, and wasted lives in the world if Satan and his demons did not exist. We have a sin nature that is capable of every kind of evil. Satan, however, plays a key role in tempting us, and should we say *yes* to his promptings, he will tighten the chains to keep us bound.

How do we resist him?

We must see all sin as our enemy, never as our friend. When faced with a moral or spiritual choice, we must understand that we cannot sin without serious consequences. We must remember that if we embrace sin, we embrace the devil. Sin is his playground; it is his trap. And if you give an inch, he will be back to take a mile.

Sometimes we are faced with a decision that does not appear to involve a clear choice between good and evil. We're talking about those rationalizations we use when the revealed will of God conflicts with our own emotions or with what seems to be best in our eyes. A woman may find herself tempted to marry a divorced man whose divorce had no biblical basis. Or, a man may convince himself it's okay to marry another woman after divorcing his wife simply on the grounds that his first marriage was not fulfilling. He fails to see the evil in his action because he feels love in his heart for his new partner. The rationalizations are legion.

Realize that you can be trapped by Satan in one single act. The mouse does not have to have a series of experiences with traps in order to be caught. Just one bite of the cheese is sufficient. Some people resist temptation for many years and yet in one act of weakness make a choice that leads them to ruin. One act of immorality or one foolish choice of a marriage partner—these and other sins have led committed believers into lives of spiritual stagnation and deterioration. Of course God is able to make the best of these situations after repentance and surrender to His will. But He cannot reverse the damage. Just ask King David.

Like Jesus, we must meet Satan by saying, "Away from me, Satan! For it is written…" (Matthew 4:10). Please notice that Jesus' quoting of Scripture did not cause Satan to flee immediately. He returned with another temptation, and then another. Luke wrote that Satan finally left "until an opportune time" (4:13). We must resist Satan repeatedly, often in a matter of a few moments. He will leave us, but be assured he will return.

Don't give up easily. Resist him, and stand firm in the faith. If you quote a verse or two and do not experience immediate results, do not doubt whether God's Word is effective. When breaking a stronghold, we must resist Satan repeatedly, perhaps for a long period of time, for he backs off only reluctantly, and always with the intent to strike again.

Understand that the best defense is the armor of God. Space forbids a detailed explanation of this armor God makes available to every

Christian (see pages 21-24, where the armor is discussed in more detail). However, you must put on this equipment every day through prayer and faith. Affirm each piece to be yours, and submit to the authority of God's Word. Satan is not invincible, only God is. In His presence, the devil is weak and cowers in fear.

Take your stand against Satan in the community of God's people, and you will be free from the grip of the evil one.

Taking God's Word to Heart

1. From what we read in 1 Peter 5:8-9, Satan is on the prowl, targeting and entrapping all who fall prey to his activities. Although he can attack from all possible angles, what do we know to be his chief point of attack?

2. What is Satan's full-time occupation? What strategies does he employ?

3. Should we let our guard down and yield to temptation, a single act may trap us. Do you know your weaknesses? In what ways can you best guard your heart and mind? Be assured that the enemy knows where to strike.

4. James tells us to resist Satan. What happens when we embrace sin? What can we do to deprive Satan of his power?

5. Read Ephesians 6:10-20. What is the "armor of God"? Discuss each piece of equipment and how it is effective in protecting us against the wiles of the devil.

THE SECOND COMING OF CHRIST

*Titus 2:13-14—While we wait for the blessed hope—
the appearing of the glory of our great God and Savior,
Jesus Christ, who gave himself for us to redeem us
from all wickedness and to purify for himself a people
that are his very own, eager to do what is good.*

*1 John 3:2-3—Dear friends, now we are children
of God, and what we will be has not yet been made
known. But we know that when Christ appears, we shall
be like him, for we shall see him as he is. All who have
this hope in him purify themselves, just as he is pure.*

Among Christians there is often disagreement about the events that surround the second coming of the Lord Jesus Christ. For example, it is our belief that the return of Christ should be seen as happening in two stages: First will come the rapture of the church, then at the end of the Great Tribulation will come the glorious return of Jesus, at which time He will judge the world and we will begin to reign with Him. Other Bible teachers are convinced that the rapture and the glorious return are the same event. But no matter what our view, we should not miss the key emphasis of the New Testament: Because Jesus is going to return, we should live holy lives in anticipation of His coming. In short, the prophecies of the Bible were not written to satisfy our curiosity about the future, but to change the way we do the business of living on earth.

In Titus 2:13-14, Paul links two ideas: the grace of God and the return of Christ. We should not interpret this verse to teach that God's grace in Christ has universally appeared to everyone, but rather that through the appearing of Christ grace is *available* to everyone. This grace, properly understood, teaches us to "say 'No' to ungodliness and worldly passions, and to live self-controlled, upright and godly lives in this present age" (verse 12). So while many people treat God's grace as though they have a license to sin, Paul taught the opposite: Grace leads to personal holiness.

How does grace lead to holiness? First, because we focus on the past, remembering the high cost of our redemption; this motivates us to want to please God from a deeply grateful heart. And second, grace promotes holy living by focusing on the future, the "blessed hope— the appearing of the glory of our great God and Savior, Jesus Christ." Every place in the New Testament where we find a reference to the return of Christ it is always linked to an appeal for holiness. The second verse above is an example of this: "Dear friends, now we are children of God, and what we will be has not yet been made known. But we know that when Christ appears, we shall be like him, for we shall see him as he is. All who have this hope in him purify themselves, just as he is pure" (1 John 3:2-3).

After Paul urged us to live in anticipation of Christ's glorious return, he went on to say that Jesus "gave himself for us to redeem us from all wickedness and to purify for himself a people that are his very own, eager to do what is good" (Titus 2:14). He shows that God's purpose in paying such a fearful price for our redemption was to purchase a holy people. When we remind ourselves of the Lord's future return, we should be motivated to pay whatever price is necessary to bring our lives in line with the holiness God desires.

Keep in mind that when Christ returns, two different events will instantly transpire. Those who have died in Christ will be raised from their graves to meet Him in the air, complete with their new, glorified, eternal bodies. And those believers who are alive at the time of His return will escape death and be similarly transformed, so that both groups will meet Him in the air. And thus we will be with the Lord forever (1 Thessalonians 4:15-17). No wonder Paul said to those who were grieving over the death of their loved ones, "Therefore encourage one another with these words" (verse 18).

Is it possible for a Christian to be embarrassed at the return of Christ? John wrote, "Dear children, continue in him, so that when he appears we may be confident and unashamed before him at his coming" (1 John 2:28). This is how we should live in light of Christ's return. Peter made a similar plea, calling our attention to the fact this earth will eventually be burned up: "The day of the Lord will come like a thief. The heavens will disappear with a roar; the elements will be destroyed by fire…Since everything will be destroyed in this way, what kind of people ought you to be? You ought to live holy and godly lives as you look forward to the day of God and speed its coming" (2 Peter 3:10-12).

It is not necessary for us to have all our questions answered about the specific details surrounding the second coming in order to anticipate this event. Nothing should generate more permanent change in our lives than the realization that Christ will one day return, and we will participate in His coming.

Let us wake up each day with the anticipation that Jesus is returning and then live with eternal values in mind. And if Jesus does not return during our lifetime, we will be resurrected to see Him when He does. Either way, today let us repent of everything that stands in the way of our total commitment to living our lives for His glory.

Time is short, and eternity is long.

Taking God's Word to Heart

1. What are the doctrines of the rapture and the second coming? What do we believe takes place during these events?

2. As we anticipate Jesus' return, what posture should we have here on earth? Are you ready for Christ's return?

3. Paul taught that grace leads to personal holiness. How does that process take place? (Read 1 John 3:2-3.)

4. When Paul spoke of Christ's return, he told the Thessalonians to "encourage one another with these words" (1 Thessalonians 4:18). What events will instantly transpire at Christ's return?

5. Why might some Christians be ashamed to stand before Christ at His coming? Read 1 John 2:28 and 2 Peter 3:11-12. Share how we can ensure our confidence to stand before Christ when He returns.

SENSUALITY

Matthew 5:27-30—*You have heard that it was said, "You shall not commit adultery." But I tell you that anyone who looks at a woman lustfully has already committed adultery with her in his heart. If your right eye causes you to stumble, gouge it out and throw it away. It is better for you to lose one part of your body than for your whole body to be thrown into hell. And if your right hand causes you to stumble, cut it off and throw it away. It is better for you to lose one part of your body than for your whole body to go into hell.*

Jesus does not let us make excuses for our passions. He plainly taught that to look upon a woman lustfully is to commit adultery in one's heart. He also knew that lust is so much a part of who we are as fallen human beings, that parting with it might just be as difficult as parting with a member of our body.

Jesus said that if our eye offends us, we should cut it out. He knew that particularly for men, lust begins with the eye. The exotic stimulation offered by pictures—whether on the big screen, television, or a computer monitor—are readily available. Next, Jesus spoke of the hand, which represents a further stage in sexual arousal, particularly for women. Tender words can easily lead to sexual stimulation and further sinful involvement. Jesus said that if the eye must be cut out or the hand cut off, so be it. For "it is better" to lose one part of your body than for your whole body "to go into hell."

Needless to say, Christ was speaking figuratively. To submit to some form of mutilation to deaden the passions of lust is not what He had in mind. Even if a man were to cut out his right eye, he could still lust with his left one. And to get rid of one's hand would hardly curb the sexual desires of the body. No, His instruction is not literal.

But there is a sense in which Christ's words are quite literally true: It would be better to lose an eye in this life than to enter hell with two. And it would be better to have one arm in heaven than enter hell with two. What Christ was saying, in the strongest possible language, is this: *Be willing to do whatever is necessary to keep from falling into sexual sin.*

Amputation is painful. We wouldn't part with our eye or hand unless it were absolutely necessary to do so. Just so, we must be willing to part with lust, even at great personal cost. Whatever form our temptation takes, we must stop the process, for it is sin sweetly poisoned.

A young man told me that throwing away the pornographic pictures he had kept stashed in his garage was difficult. His habit had become so much a part of his life that he felt as if he was throwing a part of his life away. But Jesus said, "No matter how painful it is, do it!"

Recently I (Erwin) spoke to a man who was in love with a woman who was not his wife. I explained that this relationship had to end; he had to return to his wife and rebuild his deteriorating marriage. He still had deep affection for this other woman along with feelings of "oneness" he had never known with his wife. I explained that he must end his "affair," no matter how hard it was to do so. Jesus would say, "Even though the emotional pain is excruciating, do it."

For some, removing the temptations that cause us to stumble might mean getting rid of their television set. For others it might mean cutting off friendships that lead into sin. For still others it might mean changing jobs or moving to a different location. And for all, it means accountability to other members of the body of Christ.

Too drastic? That's not as drastic as gouging out your eye or cutting off your hand! When we are not willing to take radical measures, our battle for purity is stalled. If we don't know what to do, then we should pray, "Lead us not into temptation, but deliver us from the evil one" (Matthew 6:13). We must, in all sincerity, turn to God in submission and desperation.

Amputation is painful, but it is also thorough. Benjamin Needler, a Puritan writer, put it this way: "We must not part with sin, as with a friend, with a purpose to see it again, and to have the same familiarity with it as before, or possibly greater…We must…shake our hands of it, as Paul did shake the viper off his hand into the fire."[15] Yes, we must burn every bridge behind us—and not turn back (remember Lot's wife?).

A.W. Tozer was right when he said, "That part of us that we rescue from the cross may be a very little part of us, but it is likely to be the seat of our spiritual troubles and our defeats." Our tendency is to "make provision for the flesh" by refusing to close all the doors that temptation opens for the devil's continued assault.

There is a saying that if you are going to jump across a chasm, it is much better to do it in one long jump than in two short ones. Just so, when we deal with sin in our lives, it is best that it be done thoroughly, completely, and without making it easy for us to retrace our steps.

Sexual sin, no matter how enticing, is never worth more than an arm or a leg—or worse, the sufferings of hell. Although I (Erwin) don't agree with Henry David Thoreau on most things, he was right when he said, "How prompt we are to satisfy the hunger and thirst of our bodies; how slow to satisfy the hunger and thirst of our souls."

Whatever God asks you to do, do it!

Taking God's Word to Heart

1. Read Matthew 5:27-30. Speaking in figurative terms, what is Jesus' main point in this text?

2. Notice that Jesus' condemnation of adultery went beyond the physical act to include adultery of the heart. How often do we find ourselves faced with the temptation of lust? What should be our predetermined response to lust?

3. Consider the examples given of sinful lifestyles that need

"amputation." Perhaps you can share some examples of such lifestyles. How drastic and thorough do we need to be to rid ourselves of sexual sins and sensuality?

4. Read the A.W. Tozer quote in this chapter. To what sorts of consequences do we open ourselves when we fail to close all the doors to temptation?

5. Have you ever had to cut off a sinful habit in your life? How big of a grip did that habit have on your life before you cut it out? Was the pain of getting rid of it from your life worth it?

SIN

Romans 3:23—*All have sinned and*
fall short of the glory of God.

John 8:34-36—*Jesus replied, "Very truly I tell you,*
everyone who sins is a slave to sin. Now a slave has no
permanent place in the family, but a son belongs to it
forever. So if the Son sets you free, you will be free indeed."

There was a time when the word *sin* was a strong word. When some-body used the word *sin*, we knew what they meant. Not so today because nobody sins; they just make "poor choices." Even a criminal doesn't sin; he just has a lapse in judgment. No wonder we have so many people with various neuroses. If we do not understand sin, we will not have an adequate cure for it.

Sin may be defined as any action or thought that does not conform to the holiness of God. It is disobeying God's commands. No won-der the Bible says, "All have sinned and fall short of the glory of God" (Romans 3:23). We have missed the mark; we have fallen short—far short—of God's glory. And if we have a wrong view of sin, we will have a wrong view about everything in the world that really matters. Our understanding of sin determines who we are as a person and our under-standing of God and His grace.

When we speak of original sin, we are saying that we were all born with the nature of our fallen forefather Adam. What is more, his sin is imputed to us—that is, it is reckoned to our account. Initially that might appear to be unfair, but just imagine being born into a family that is heavily in debt. Although you had nothing to do with the family's misuse of funds, you inherit their indebtedness. While it's true we were not in the Garden of Eden when Adam and Eve sinned, we all have felt the effects of their sin and our own. Ever since Adam and Eve fell into sin, every child is born a sinner and therefore is a potential criminal. At the time of birth, the nature of Adolf Hitler was essentially no different than the nature of Mother Teresa.

Because we ourselves are fallen, we can't fully comprehend the horrors of sin. We often think of sin as the outward transgressions of adultery, theft, and the like, and forget that sin is essentially the thoughts and attitudes of the soul. William Farley writes, "Remember, all Adam and Eve did was to bite into a forbidden apple. They didn't commit adultery or snort cocaine. Yet the result was death, suffering, alienation, and rejection for billions. Can we fully comprehend the horror of sin? Is it possible for us to ever see God in perspective?"[16]

We don't realize the extent to which sin deceives us because those very deceptions lie undetected, just beyond the range of our perceptions. An inadequate view of sin leads to an inadequate understanding of the need for the gospel. In their book *How People Change*, Timothy Lane and Paul David Tripp wrote, "One of the reasons teenagers are not excited by the gospel is that they think they do not need it. Many parents have successfully raised self-righteous little Pharisees. When they look at themselves, they do not see a sinner in desperate need, so they are not grateful for a Savior."[17]

A shallow view of sin causes us to create a wrong view of God; without much effort we soon imagine a god who exists only in our imaginations. If our sins are deemed to be small, God will be seen as tolerant and accommodating. On a plane, a woman said to a friend of ours, "If God doesn't accept me, then I am going to tell Him to lighten up." In other words, "My sins aren't that great; if God knows what He is doing, He will understand my predicament and welcome me into whatever paradise exists." I've heard Christians say essentially the same thing: "Okay, so I sin. God knows I'm human; I'm not as bad as some other people I know."

Sin makes us hide our true selves from ourselves. We become defensive, secretive, and quick to justify ourselves to others. We see other people's sins more clearly than we do our own. And we live with an inflated view of our own goodness. We don't have to be good, but it is important for us to appear good to others.

Left unchecked, this tolerant view of sin will entice us to live our lives in two compartments. In World A we might be a Sunday school teacher, a deacon, and well respected in the community. In World B we might be a wife-beater, an alcoholic, a child abuser, or—heaven forbid—a child molester. World A and world B are never allowed to come together. In fact, we put up a soundproof wall between them so that we can live with ourselves. Like one man said, "There was a part of my mind where no one, not even God, was allowed to enter." In this way, we can easily build our whole lives on deceptions and lies.

We are also frequently deceived about the long-term consequences of sin. We tell ourselves that we can handle sin's effects, and we figure that as long as we are not addicted, we are quite fine, thank you. We end up filling our lives with enough small pleasures to hide the emptiness that sin has brought into our lives. And we forget that to be at peace with our sin is to be at war with God, and that to love God is to hate sin.

Sin dulls our spiritual appetite. It dulls our interest in God and causes us to approach Him on our own terms. We come to Him for relief from our guilt, but not to pursue holiness.

In our unconverted state, we are "dead in…transgressions and sins" (Ephesians 2:1). Like a corpse in a funeral home, we cannot raise ourselves; we cannot respond to commands to come alive. God must intervene, come to our rescue, and save us.

All of us have a dark side. Read carefully what Lewis B. Smedes wrote: "Our inner lives are not partitioned like day and night, with pure light on one side of us and total darkness on the other. Mostly our souls are shadowed places. We live at the border where our dark sides block our light and throw a shadow over our interior places. We cannot always tell where our light ends and our shadow begins or where our shadow ends and our darkness begins."[18] And, we might add, we cannot change our own nature. The prophet Jeremiah asked, "Can a leopard change its spots?" (see Jeremiah 13:23). The answer, of course, is *no*. You might as well try to convince a tiger to eat straw as to convince an unconverted person that he should love God and hate his sin.

Just as a corpse cannot feel pain, so sin makes us insensitive to the reality of who we are; we are unable to feel the impact our sin has on God and others. We are so adept at rationalizing our thoughts and actions and tweaking our image that we refuse to take an honest look deep within ourselves with the help of the Holy Spirit. Sin hardens the heart and makes us justify what we intuitively know is wrong, and yes, evil.

Thankfully, God comes to the cemetery and speaks words that cause us to be resurrected to new life. If you have never been born again—that is, if God has never made you alive—throw yourself upon His mercy. He will save you from your sin and from yourself.

Only Jesus can rescue us from sin's deceptive bondage.

Taking God's Word to Heart

1. What are some of the world's definitions for *sin*? Read Romans 3:23. What is the biblical definition of sin?

2. Theologians refer to what is called "original sin." What is it, and how are we all affected by it?

3. What do we mean when we say someone has a shallow view of sin? What can a shallow view of sin cause in our lives?

4. How is it we are deceived about the long-term consequences of sin? Have you ever underestimated the impact of a sin in your life, only to find its consequences more severe than you had imagined? Explain.

5. Sin can dull our spiritual appetite. How can it change our approach to God and holiness?

TEMPTATION

1 Corinthians 10:13—*No temptation has overtaken you except what is common to mankind. And God is faithful; he will not let you be tempted beyond what you can bear. But when you are tempted, he will also provide a way out so that you can endure it.*

James 1:13-15—*When tempted, no one should say, "God is tempting me." For God cannot be tempted by evil, nor does he tempt anyone; but each one is tempted when they are dragged away by their own evil desire and enticed. Then, after desire has conceived, it gives birth to sin; and sin, when it is full-grown, gives birth to death.*

Temptation might be defined as the desire to satisfy a legitimate need in an illegitimate or sinful way. Temptations take many forms: dishonesty for financial gain, the urge for revenge motivated by anger or fueled by the desire to get even, a lie told to give a wrong impression. Some people are driven by their ego to excel for the sake of recognition and fame. The lusts of the flesh include immorality, addictions (sexual, substance, pornography, gambling), greed, pride, and so on. And, like throwing a piece of meat to an angry tiger, the more these urges are fed, the stronger they become, hungry for more.

Satan is not so much interested in what sin we yield to; his greater purpose is to separate us from fellowship with our heavenly Father. He hates the fact there are people who actually love God so much that they are willing to say *no* to his enticements in favor of God's fellowship and blessing. When temptation arises, God wants to bring out the best in us, whereas Satan wants to bring out the worst. And when we yield to temptation, the result is remorse, regret, and God's discipline. By contrast, when we say *no* to the appetites that lead us to sin, we bring glory to God. But the only way we can overcome temptation is to develop a passion for Christ that is greater than our passion to sin.

So how can we say no to temptation?

First, whenever possible, we must remove ourselves from the path of temptation. When Paul wrote to his adopted son Timothy, he said, "Flee from all this, and pursue righteousness, godliness, faith, love, endurance and gentleness. Fight the good fight of the faith" (1 Timothy 6:11-12). Paul was saying, "Stay away from the environments that draw you toward sin, and instead, make the pursuit of pleasing God your highest priority." Jesus put it even more strongly, saying that if our eye causes us to stumble, we should "gouge it out" (Matthew 5:29).

Of course Jesus didn't mean that literally; rather, He meant we should do whatever is necessary to keep us from the lusts of the eyes. Our problem, quite frankly, is that we often *want* to be tempted and even *plan* to be tempted. Sometimes we just need to take drastic action and remove ourselves from the place where we know we will be tempted. Paul put it this way: "Put on the Lord Jesus Christ, and make no provision for the flesh, to gratify its desires" (Romans 13:14 ESV).

Even resigning from a job because it places us in the vicinity of temptation is not too great a price to pay for obedience to Christ. I (Erwin) was talking with a married man who was falling in love with a woman at work, and told him he should quit his position rather than jeopardize his marriage. He responded, "But I have to earn a living!" Unfortunately, he did not take my advice, and you can already predict what happened. He kept his job, but destroyed his marriage—a terrible bargain indeed. Yes, we do have to earn a living, but it would be better to go hungry than fall into an immoral relationship. Whenever possible, we should run—not walk—from the temptations that lurk nearby.

Second, and more importantly, we must see Jesus as having won a victory on our behalf. His death on the cross did not just mean that

Satan was officially defeated; it also meant that we who believe on Christ are no longer Satan's subjects. We are now under a new owner. At one time we belonged to the kingdom of darkness, enslaved by our sins; but our new allegiance is to Jesus. In other words, we have a new Master. No matter how overwhelming a temptation seems, there is a way of escape, if only we are willing to take it (1 Corinthians 10:13). And equally important is that we must be willing to seek freedom from the relentless demands that our desires be satisfied.

Third, we must follow the example of Jesus, who knew the Scripture passages He needed to successfully fight against Satan. We must memorize, in advance, verses that speak directly to the temptations we know we will face. Some verses can be used for any temptation—for example, a verse we use often is 1 Peter 1:15-16: "Just as he who called you is holy, so be holy in all you do; for it is written: 'Be holy, because I am holy.'"

Finally, fellowship with other Christians is essential. Confessing our need in the presence of those we trust and asking them for their prayer support is often the way to deliverance. I (Erwin) have told men who struggle with pornography that they can fall into that pit alone, but they can't get out of it alone. We cannot live the Christian life in isolation from other believers. A key help in overcoming temptation is the prayers, personal encouragement, and accountability of those who are a part of the body of Christ.

There is an old story of an Indian who described the war within his heart as two dogs fighting each other. "There is a dark, angry dog who fights from the shadows; then there is a good dog who fights in the light."

"Which one wins?" he was asked.

"The one I feed the most."

When we make a genuine effort to overcome temptation, we prove that we love God more than we love our sin.

Taking God's Word to Heart

1. Define *temptation*. What forms can temptation take?

2. When it comes to temptation, what is Satan's purpose? What happens when we yield to his temptations and help fulfill his purpose? What happens when we say no to temptation?

3. Read 1 Timothy 6:11-12 and Romans 13:14. What step does Romans 13:14 suggest we take to overcome temptation?

4. What confidence does Christ's death on the cross give us for overcoming temptation? Will we ever face a temptation so overwhelming that there is no way of escape? What might a way of escape look like?

5. Note that Jesus answered Satan's temptations with Scripture. How effectively can you resist the devil when you memorize Scripture in advance of being tempted? What plan are you using to memorize and hide God's Word in your heart? Where is there room for improvement?

THANKSGIVING

1 Thessalonians 5:16-18—*Rejoice always, pray continually, give thanks in all circumstances; for this is God's will for you in Christ Jesus.*

Psalm 50:23—*Those who sacrifice thank offerings honor me, and to the blameless I will show my salvation.*

Giving thanks changes everything.

If you've never experienced the power of thanksgiving, you may soon be experiencing an attitude adjustment. When we read, "Give thanks in all circumstances," we might find ourselves tempted to hurry past this exhortation, thinking that giving thanks at all times is either impractical or irrelevant. We might even think we have very little for which to give thanks. It is difficult to give thanks when you have been laid off from your job, your spouse tells you he or she is leaving, or you've been told you have a terminal disease. Yet that is exactly what Paul taught—we are to give thanks in all circumstances—the bad and the good, the promotions and the demotions.

Now, there is a difference between giving praise and expressing thanks. *Praise* honors God for who He is by focusing on His attributes, whereas thanksgiving honors God for what He has done. We offer praise because of His power, love, and justice; and we offer thanksgiving for the blessings that surround us, including those that are hard and difficult to accept.

In fact, thanksgiving is a game-changer. Why? First, because it honors God by reaffirming His sovereignty. When we thank Him for all things—both good and bad—we affirm that He is in charge of all the affairs that take place in His universe. No, we do not give thanks for evil per se; rather, we give thanks for how God will use evil to further His own purposes and thereby bring glory to Himself. In thanksgiving we not only affirm that God *is* good, but also that He *does* good by giving us underserved blessings and bringing us hope even in the midst of chaos and evil.

Second, thanksgiving changes us. When we give thanks for everything, faith is built in our hearts; the weight of our burdens is lifted because we affirm those burdens are God's, not ours. We've discovered that giving thanks for setbacks gives us a new perspective; it frees us to see difficulties as a part of a larger purpose. And it also frees us up to worship God, to remind ourselves of His greatness, love, and providence.

How can you learn to practice thanksgiving every day of your life?

First, turn every complaint into a reason to give thanks to God. Matthew Henry, a writer from a previous generation, was robbed one evening. That night he wrote in his diary, "I am thankful that he took just my wallet and not my life; I am thankful that even though he took all I had, that wasn't much; I am thankful that I was the one who was robbed and not the robber!"

On 9/11, Lisa Beamer's husband, Todd, shouted, "Let's roll!" in an attempt to stop hijackers from commandeering United Airlines Flight 93 (which went on to crash into a field in Pennsylvania). Later, on her husband's birthday, Lisa was feeling sorry for herself as a widow. Her eight-year-old son, David, asked why she felt so sad, and she said, "Because Daddy isn't with us on his birthday." To which David replied, "But, Mom, we can still have cake, can't we?"[19]

Yes, when the bottom falls out of our lives, when we feel as if everything is against us, we still have things for which we can be thankful. We can still connect with friends; we can still go to church; we are still alive. We can still eat cake.

Second, begin the day by giving thanks to God for all the things you are sincerely thankful for. As you continue this practice, you will soon find yourself increasing the number of things for which you can give thanks—your list will graduate from the obvious to the less obvious. Eventually you will start giving thanks for a difficult co-worker, for a lack of funds, and even for difficult health issues. Thanksgiving will become so much a part of your attitude that it will become a natural response to the circumstances of life.

About 15 years ago a relatively young man who had been strong and healthy was reduced to an invalid by a massive stroke. Visiting him took great patience because he spoke so slowly. He found it difficult to pronounce words, and his conversation was limited to the effects of his illness and his meager surroundings. Immediately after the stroke he was bitter, angry with God over what he saw as an unnecessary tragedy. But over the years, he had a change of heart. He now says, "I give thanks every day for what happened. Beforehand, I had both the money and the desire to enjoy a sinful lifestyle. This tragedy has kept me from that. Yes, I thank God for *this*."

Right now, give thanks to God for everything—the sorrows as well as the joys, the negatives as well as the positives, the pain as well as the pleasure. You can't turn bad news into good news simply by giving thanks, but you *can* make the bad news more bearable. You *can* honor God and free yourself from complaining and anxiety.

Indeed, you will discover that thanksgiving changes everything.

Taking God's Word to Heart

1. What exactly does Paul mean when he says to give thanks in all circumstances? Does that include both good and bad circumstances? Why do you think that's the case?

2. What is the difference between *praise* and *thanksgiving*? For what reasons do we offer each to God?

3. Why is the act of giving thanks so important? What does it affirm and reaffirm regarding God's sovereignty?

4. How does giving thanks to God impact us? Discuss the chapter's insights on this aspect of giving thanks.

5. How do you approach giving thanks in all circumstances? What are some ways you can make thanksgiving part of your daily attitude and natural response to circumstances?

THE WILL OF GOD

*1 Thessalonians 4:3-5—It is God's will that you
should be sanctified: that you should avoid sexual
immorality; that each of you should learn to control your
own body in a way that is holy and honorable, not in
passionate lust like the pagans, who do not know God.*

*1 Thessalonians 5:16-18—Rejoice always, pray
continually, give thanks in all circumstances; for
this is God's will for you in Christ Jesus.*

Every Christian has been faced with this dilemma: How can I know God's will for my life? Where should I attend college? Whom shall I marry? What vocation should I pursue? Where shall I live? And the list of such questions is endless.

For openers, we need to understand that God takes delight in guiding His children. We should not think that God is in heaven presenting us with a number of options and then daring us to choose the right one. The will of God is not a mystery wrapped in an enigma.

Most importantly, the will of God is first and foremost about knowing God and doing what He has asked us to do. And here is the key: *If we are obedient to what God has revealed, He is obligated to guide us in matters He has not revealed.* In other words, knowing God's will is first and foremost presented in Scripture as walking closely with Him; to know Him is to please Him by our inner devotion and personal obedience. Guidance follows.

Reread the above verses. Only when we pursue these commands are we ready to seek God's will about other matters. All of us have an "internal DVD" that we replay in our minds which captures the life we want: a happy marriage, a beautiful home, the recognition and the luxury and early retirement—all of that has to be given to God. Our ambitions just might be canceled when we honestly are willing to do whatever God asks. We can't say, "God, please give me a preview of what You have in mind for my life so that I can choose whether or not I like it."

When you are faced with an important decision, weigh your priorities. Take a sheet of paper and write down the pros and the cons, paying careful attention to what this decision will mean to you, your family, and your personal fulfillment. The job that pays the most isn't necessarily the one that is best for you. Many a person has sacrificed what is most important for that which is of lesser importance. So you have to ask hard questions—questions such as, What does this decision mean for my emotional and spiritual health? What impact will it have on my family? Will I be expected to compromise my personal convictions? Am I doing this just to bolster my status, or is there a more noble, eternal reason I'm making this particular choice?

Whenever you can, you'll want to trade success for significance. D.L. Moody, the founder of the church at which we serve, had the ambition to become the most successful salesman in Chicago, but God changed Moody's mind when he heard a group of Sunday school girls pray for their dying teacher. Moody said money could never tempt him again. He saw the larger picture, and that motivated him to increase his work among the poor children of Chicago. Eventually he went on to become one of the most prominent evangelists in the world. Of course, we're not suggesting that any of us should try to follow in his footsteps. Rather, we are simply saying it is better to choose significance over success—to choose that which counts for eternity.

With that in mind, here is a promise we can claim: "Let the peace of Christ rule in your hearts, since as members of one body you were called to peace. And be thankful" (Colossians 3:15). That word "rule" means that peace is like an umpire that should control our hearts, giving us a thumbs up or a thumbs down in response to what we are doing or are about to do. At the end of the day, we should be convinced that what we are doing is right and good, and in harmony with what God wants.

The peace of God sits in judgment of our lifestyles and decisions. Sometimes there is what we could call a "check in our spirit"—that is, a hunch that we are about to embark on the wrong path. We should listen to this prompting from the Holy Spirit, especially if we have a suspicion that something isn't right. All Christians are indwelt by the Holy Spirit, whom we grieve when we sin and take wrong paths. By contrast, when we obey God, the Spirit brings us peace.

Frequently we cannot foresee the consequences of our decisions, but God can. And that is why it is so important not only to consult God, but also to be quiet enough in our inner being so that a still small voice can speak to us when we are about to make a mistake. We've all had the experience of sensing that there is a cloud over a decision we are about to make. When that happens, I've learned to back off and ask, What am I missing in this decision? Women often have a keener sense of intuition than men. When they sense that something is amiss, we who are husbands would do well to listen and consider what they have to say to us.

There is, of course, a danger in relying on inner peace alone as our guide. People have made the most bizarre decisions on the basis that they had "a peace about it." We can talk ourselves into having peace; we can rationalize that we are at peace; and eventually our emotions will end up following the path our minds have insisted on. Wise friends can help us keep on the right track.

Sometimes circumstances dictate what our next steps should be; or, sometimes people give us guidance by sharing their wisdom or putting us in touch with others who become a part of our decision. Often there is a confluence of events that lead us toward the strong conviction that God is putting a scenario together for us that will introduce us to new possibilities.

We've discovered that God has often guided us when we have not even been aware of it. We would walk through one door of opportunity that seemed reasonable to us, and that would lead to yet another open door, and then only in retrospect were we able to see how important those initial and ordinary decisions were.

When knowing God is our first priority, we will find ourselves able to make our decisions with greater confidence and peace.

Taking God's Word to Heart

1. Have you grappled with finding the will of God for important decisions in your life? Share your struggles and successes.

2. If we understand that the will of God is first and foremost about knowing God and doing what He has asked of us, what then is the key? How important is it that we obey what has been revealed to us in Scripture?

3. How have you approached important life decisions in the past? Look again at what the chapter says about carefully weighing priorities. What are the steps of this process? Drawing from your experience, can you include additional steps that could be helpful to others?

4. Colossians 3:15 gives us a promise we can claim as we work out God's will in our lives. Look carefully at this passage. What is significant about the word "rule"?

5. In addition to inner peace, what are other God-directed influences we can look to for guidance in making our decisions?

WITNESSING

Matthew 5:14,16—*You are the light of the world...*
let your light shine before others, that they may see
your good deeds and glorify your Father in heaven.

1 Peter 3:15—*In your hearts revere Christ as Lord.*
Always be prepared to give an answer to everyone
who asks you to give the reason for the hope that you
have. But do this with gentleness and respect.

We are living at a time of increased interest in what is popularly called spirituality without a belief in specific doctrines. People are trying to connect with something or someone that is greater than they are, but they are skeptical of a solution that will make them admit their sin and turn to God in humble repentance. Quite apart from whether we deserve it or not, we as Christians are viewed as narrow-minded, judgmental, and a detriment to progress. The Jesus of the Sermon on the Mount enjoys a wonderful reputation, but the Jesus of the cross and resurrection is ignored and denied.

How do we let our light shine in a world where people are comfortable in their moral and spiritual darkness? We deeply believe that we have a great opportunity to impact our culture, and more importantly, to change the spiritual direction of those who are within our sphere of influence. We have the privilege of living at a time when millions of seekers are trying to find their way amid a blizzard of religious options. If we are sensitive to human needs, we will soon learn that many people are seeking fulfillment, and that may bring us the privilege of helping them on their spiritual journey.

Our present challenge is like that of the early Christians, who lived in a culture driven by a passionate commitment to spirituality. Emperor worship, along with a myriad of gods and goddesses, dominated Roman culture and thought. The pagans were willing to add Jesus to the long list of gods that people could worship. But what they could not tolerate was the idea there is only one true God who declares that all other rivals are worthless idols. In other words, the pagans said it was okay for Jesus to be a god, but they took offense at the Christian teaching that Jesus was King of kings and Lord of lords.

How do we witness to people today who have that same mind-set?

First, people must actually see the light. We must avoid being obnoxious, but at the same time we also must avoid keeping our mouths closed. We've discovered the best way to share our faith is by asking questions, by finding out where others are on their spiritual journey. We do what we can to invite discussion, and we take the time to listen to what others are thinking about God, religion, and Jesus in particular.

How is this done? Here are some questions we've used to begin or carry on a spiritual conversation:

- Where are you on your spiritual journey?

- What do you think about Jesus?

- How much adult consideration have you given to the Bible?

- How do you understand the idea of God?

- What has been your experience, if any, with Christianity?

- Would you mind if I were to share with you something that someone once shared with me that changed my life?

- I'd love to pray for you. Do you have anything you'd like me to pray about over the next couple of weeks?

If you look at the Gospels, you'll notice that Jesus carried on dialogue with people around Him by asking questions. A further step we've taken is to give a friend or colleague a book to read, saying, "I think you'll enjoy reading this. Could we meet again to discuss it in a few weeks?" The book itself might or might not be gospel-centered; what we want to do initially is to open up dialogue. Other books can follow later.

We must also learn, as best we can, how to defend what we believe. Many Christians feel intimidated about sharing their faith because they think they need to know all the answers before getting into a discussion. But in today's religious climate, being a good listener is more important than being a good talker. People want to be heard. And listening to what they say and feel is the first step to building a bridge that leads to their hearts.

And what should you do if you encounter hostility? Befriend the person and ask why he or she is so angry toward or turned off by Christianity. Many people have, humanly speaking, good reason to regard us with skepticism and distrust. True friendship is still the best means of evangelism. One reason the early church was so successful is that they practiced the art of hospitality. Their kindness reached the world.

Finally, and perhaps most important of all, we ourselves must live in the light. Think of how hollow our witness is when we are not living authentically—that is, living with the heart of a servant, and living with integrity. Notice that Jesus said those who live in darkness should see our good works and glorify the Father who is in heaven. Good deeds, perhaps, even more than good words, give credibility to the light.

We also must remember that only God can open the human heart and draws sinners to Himself. Our responsibility is to share the message; it is God's responsibility to supply the enablement to respond to the knowledge that has been imparted. As Jesus put it, "No one can come to me unless the Father who sent me draws them, and I will raise them up at the last day" (John 6:44).

God will not hold us accountable if others do not believe the gospel; rather, He will hold us accountable if we do not share the gospel with others. Our responsibility is to sow the seed, and His responsibility is to prepare the soil of the human heart to receive it. Only He can grant the faith needed to believe the gospel.

Courageous and loving witnessing with regard to our faith is the great need of the hour!

Taking God's Word to Heart

1. Compare what is typically known today as "popular spirituality" with true biblical spirituality. Upon what is each grounded? Why might people have an increased interest in popular spirituality?

2. How do we impact a lost world that is too comfortable in their spiritual darkness? How can we get the attention of a culture that does not generally respect the gospel message?

3. One way to engage the lost is by asking them questions that focus on their spiritual journey. Review questions listed in the chapter. What are some other questions you have used in your witnessing encounters?

4. Another key aspect of witnessing to the lost is being able to defend your Christian beliefs. Are you able to give a reason for your faith? What are among the things you can say?

5. It's vital for the lost to see authentic Christianity in action, for that serves as a living testimony in the midst of our dark culture. What happens when we shine our light in the darkness?

THE WORD OF GOD

Hebrews 4:12—The word of God is living and active.
Sharper than any double-edged sword, it penetrates
even to dividing soul and spirit, joints and marrow;
it judges the thoughts and attitudes of the heart.

Psalm 119:105—Your word is a lamp
for my feet, a light on my path.

Imagine you are driving on a dimly lit street in a bad neighborhood in Los Angeles. You accidently drive over a sharp metal object, and two of your tires go flat. As you contemplate your next move, a dozen young men spill out of a nearby building and strut toward you. You can already see yourself being dragged from the car, robbed, and beaten. Would it make a difference if you were to discover that these young men were on their way home from a Bible study? Such news would make even an atheist feel better!

One of the many reasons we believe the Bible is the Word of God is because of its power. We should not be surprised that God's Word is compared to a sword. The ancient Roman soldier's sword had two edges so that it could cut both ways. The Word of God is "sharper than any double-edged sword" such that it can dissect us and help us discern who we truly are and what we must do to establish a relationship with God. It wounds us that it might heal us.

The Word of God is also "living and active"—it is not just words on a page. The words are empowered by God because they come with His authority and blessing. Wherever the Word of God is, the Spirit is present to make the words relevant, filled with power and life. In fact, the apostle Peter said, "You have been born again, not of perishable seed, but of imperishable, through the living and enduring word of God" (1 Peter 1:23).

The Bible differs from a two-edged sword in this respect: It is sharper than such a sword could ever be! In the original Greek text we find the word *tomoteros*, which comes from the Greek word *temno*, which means "to cut." It is the language of surgery, the language of dissection. To quote Greek scholar Marvin R. Vincent, "The form of expression is poetical, and signifies that the word penetrates to the inmost recesses of our spiritual being as a sword cuts through the joints and marrow of the body. The separation is not of one part from the other, but operates in each department of the spiritual nature."[20] The Word of God goes through both the soul and spirit; it goes through both the joints and marrow. It stops at nothing until it comes to reality. In the presence of this book, there can be no pretense.

God's Word is also able to judge "the thoughts and attitudes of the heart." To "judge" means to "sift out" and "analyze as evidence." The Bible sits in judgment of all the activity of the soul and spirit. It separates base motives from noble ones; it distinguishes between that which is of the flesh and that which is of the Spirit.

More specifically, the Word judges our "thoughts"—that is, the things we ponder. It judges our reflections—what we think as we drive along the expressway; what we think about other people, whether pleasant or unpleasant. Thousands of thoughts course through our minds each day. The Word of God monitors these musings moment by moment.

Not only our thoughts are judged, but also our "attitudes." This refers to the origin of our thoughts—the conceptions of the past and the intentions of the future are equally known. Greek scholar Kenneth Wuest translates this last phrase as saying that the Word of God "is able to penetrate into the furthermost recesses of a person's spiritual being, sifting out and analyzing the thoughts and intents of the heart."[21]

The author of Hebrews goes on to say, "Nothing in all creation is hidden from God's sight. Everything is uncovered and laid bare before the eyes of him to whom we must give account" (4:13). Imagine here a cadaver laid out on a table, with every sinew, every nerve, and every particle of bone and flesh laid bare.

Let's not miss the connection between verses 12 and 13! The author of Hebrews passes easily from talking about God's spoken Word to God's incarnate Word (Christ). Obviously he wants us to understand that we are laid bare before the eyes of Christ. The Word of God, like an X-ray machine, reveals who we really are, and Christ examines the X-ray plates carefully, noting every speck that appears on them.

To put it differently: We lie on God's surgical table. The Word of God has separated reality from fantasy, right from wrong, the pure from the tainted. In this spiritual autopsy, there is, figuratively speaking, a tumor here, a diseased cell there, and a bone that has a hairline fracture. Every aspiration, every mental and emotional component is dissected, until at last the truth about us has been revealed.

Of course, as we mentioned, the Word of God not only cuts us open, but it also heals us. Through God's Word we are cleansed, healed, comforted, and transformed. No wonder David wrote of the righteous person, "[His] delight is in the law of the LORD, and on his law he meditates day and night. He is like a tree planted by streams of water that yields its fruit in season, and its leaf does not wither. In all that he does, he prospers" (Psalm 1:2-3).

Clearly, then, the practice of meditating on God's Word should be our most important daily discipline.

Taking God's Word to Heart

1. How do you explain the power of God's Word? Why is the Bible's power described as that of a two-edged sword?

2. Read 1 Peter 1:23. In what ways is the Word of God alive? How does the Holy Spirit use the Word to minister to us?

3. In Hebrews 4, we learn that the Word of God judges the

thoughts and attitudes of our hearts. In what ways does the Bible judge our thoughts and attitudes?

4. Read Psalm 1:2-3. What does this powerful passage describe? How does the Word of God heal us? How does it nourish our inner being?

5. Compare the written Word of God with the Incarnate Word of God (John 1:1,14). What do both reveal to us?

Part 2:

ADDITIONAL BIBLE MEMORY VERSES FOR THE TOPICS IN THIS BOOK

ADDITIONAL BIBLE MEMORY VERSES

"Sanctify them by the truth; Your word is truth" (John 17:17).

It is our hope that you are already on your way toward memorizing the Bible verses in this book. If you would like to commit additional Scripture passages to memory, we've compiled a list of them here. All the topics in this book are listed below. The first verse under each topic heading is preceded by an asterisk (*), which indicates that is the theme verse for that topic earlier in this book. Below each theme verse are other passages you can use to further benefit from the life-changing power of God's Word.

Adversity

*Psalm 46:1—God is our refuge and strength, an ever-present help in trouble.

1 Peter 1:6-7—In this you greatly rejoice, though now for a little while you may have had to suffer grief in all kinds of trials. These have come so that the proven genuineness of your faith—of greater worth than gold, which perishes even though refined by fire—may result in praise, glory and honor when Jesus Christ is revealed.

1 Peter 4:19—Those who suffer according to God's will should commit themselves to their faithful Creator and continue to do good.

1 Peter 5:10—The God of all grace, who called you to his eternal glory in Christ, after you have suffered a little while, will himself restore you and make you strong, firm and steadfast.

James 1:2-4—Consider it pure joy, my brothers and sisters, whenever you face trials of many kinds, because you know that the testing of your faith produces perseverance. Let perseverance finish its work so that you may be mature and complete, not lacking anything.

Psalm 119:75-76—I know, Lord, that your laws are righteous, and that in faithfulness you have afflicted me. May your unfailing love be my comfort, according to your promise to your servant.

Anxiety

Matthew 6:33-34—Seek first his kingdom and his righteousness, and all these things will be given to you as well. Therefore do not worry about tomorrow, for tomorrow will worry about itself. Each day has enough trouble of its own.

Philippians 4:6-7—Do not be anxious about anything, but in every situation, by prayer and petition, with thanksgiving, present your requests to God. And the peace of God, which transcends all understanding, will guard your hearts and your minds in Christ Jesus.

1 Peter 5:6-7—Humble yourselves, therefore, under God's mighty hand, that he may lift you up in due time. Cast all your anxiety on him because he cares for you.

Psalm 37:3-8—Trust in the Lord and do good; dwell in the land and enjoy safe pasture. Take delight in the Lord, and he will give you the desires of your heart. Commit your way to the Lord; trust in him and he will do this: He will make your righteous reward shine like the dawn, your vindication like the noonday sun. Be still before the Lord and wait patiently for him; do not fret when people succeed in their ways, when they carry out their wicked schemes. Refrain from anger and turn from wrath; do not fret—it leads only to evil.

Isaiah 41:10—Do not fear, for I am with you; do not be dismayed, for I am your God. I will strengthen you and help you; I will uphold you with my righteous right hand.

Armor of God

Ephesians 6:10-11—Be strong in the Lord and in his mighty power. Put on the full armor of God, so that you can take your stand against the devil's schemes.

Ephesians 6:12-17—Our struggle is not against flesh and blood, but against the rulers, against the authorities, against the powers of this dark world and against the spiritual forces of evil in the heavenly realms. Therefore put on the full armor of God, so that when the day of evil comes, you may be able to stand your ground, and after you have done everything, to stand. Stand firm then, with the belt of truth buckled around your waist, with the breastplate of righteousness in place, and with your feet fitted with the readiness that comes from the gospel of peace. In addition to all this, take up the shield of faith, with which you can extinguish all the flaming arrows of the evil one. Take the helmet of salvation and the sword of the Spirit, which is the word of God.

Ephesians 1:18-21—I pray that the eyes of your heart may be enlightened in order that you may know...his incomparably great power for us who believe. That power is the same as the mighty strength he exerted when he raised Christ from the dead and seated him at his right hand in the heavenly realms, far above all rule and authority, power and dominion, and every name that is invoked, not only in the present age but also in the one to come.

2 Timothy 2:3-4—Join with me in suffering, like a good soldier of Christ Jesus. No one serving as a soldier gets entangled in civilian affairs, but rather tries to please his commanding officer.

Assurance

Romans 8:15-16—The Spirit you received does not make you slaves, so that you live in fear again; rather, the Spirit you received brought about your adoption to sonship. And by him we cry, "*Abba*, Father." The Spirit himself testifies with our spirit that we are God's children.

1 John 5:13—I write these things to you who believe in the name of the Son of God so that you may know that you have eternal life.

John 10:27-30—My sheep listen to my voice; I know them, and they follow me. I give them eternal life, and they shall never perish; no one will snatch them out of my hand. My Father, who has given them to me, is greater than all; no one can snatch them out of my Father's hand. I and the Father are one.

1 John 3:1-3—See what great love the Father has lavished on us, that we should be called children of God! And that is what we are! The reason the world does not know us is that it did not know him. Dear friends, now we are children of God, and what we will be has not yet been made known. But we know that when Christ appears, we shall be like him, for we shall see him as he is. All who have this hope in him purify themselves, just as he is pure.

Character/Integrity

*Psalm 15:1-2—LORD, who may dwell in your sacred tent? Who may live on your holy mountain? The one whose walk is blameless, who does what is righteous, who speaks the truth from their heart.

Proverbs 4:23—Above all else, guard your heart, for everything you do flows from it.

Job 5:17-18—Blessed is the one whom God corrects; so do not despise the discipline of the Almighty. For he wounds, but he also binds up; he injures, but his hands also heal.

Romans 7:23-25—I see another law at work in me, waging war against the law of my mind and making me a prisoner of the law of sin at work within me. What a wretched man I am! Who will rescue me from this body that is subject to death? Thanks be to God, who delivers me through Jesus Christ our Lord! So then, I myself in my mind am a slave to God's law, but in my sinful nature a slave to the law of sin.

2 Corinthians 5:17—If anyone is in Christ, the new creation has come: the old has gone, the new is here!

Philippians 2:14-15—Do everything without grumbling or arguing, so that you may become blameless and pure, "children of God without fault in a warped and crooked generation." Then you will shine among them like stars in the sky.

Conscience

Hebrews 10:22—Let us draw near to God with a sincere heart and with the full assurance that faith brings, having our hearts sprinkled to cleanse us from a guilty conscience and having our bodies washed with pure water.

1 John 3:21-22—Dear friends, if our hearts do not condemn us, we have confidence before God and receive from him anything we ask, because we keep his commands and do what pleases him.

Hebrews 9:14—How much more, then, will the blood of Christ, who through the eternal Spirit offered himself unblemished to God, cleanse our consciences from acts that lead to death, so that we may serve the living God!

1 John 3:18-23—Dear children, let us not love with words or speech but with actions and in truth. This is how we know that we belong to the truth and how we set our hearts at rest in his presence: If our hearts condemn us, we know that God is greater than our hearts, and he knows everything. Dear friends, if our hearts do not condemn us, we have confidence before God and receive from him anything we ask, because we keep his commands and do what pleases him. And this is his command: to believe in the name of his Son, Jesus Christ, and to love one another as he commanded us.

Courage

Joshua 1:7-9—Be strong and very courageous. Be careful to obey all the law my servant Moses gave you; do not turn from it to the right or to the left, that you may be successful wherever you go. Keep this Book of the Law always on your lips; meditate on it day and night, so that you may be careful to do everything written in it. Then you will be prosperous and successful. Have I not commanded you? Be strong and courageous. Do not be afraid; do not be discouraged, for the LORD your God will be with you wherever you go.

Psalm 27:13-14—I remain confident of this: I will see the goodness of the LORD in the land of the living. Wait for the LORD; be strong and take heart and wait for the LORD.

Psalm 33:18-22—The eyes of the LORD are on those who fear him, on those whose hope is in his unfailing love, to deliver them from death and keep them alive in famine. We wait in hope for the LORD; he is our help and our shield. In him our hearts rejoice, for we trust in his holy name. May your unfailing love be with us, LORD, even as we put our hope in you.

Hebrews 13:20-21—May the God of peace, who through the blood of the eternal covenant brought back from the dead our Lord Jesus, that great Shepherd of the sheep, equip you with everything good for doing his will, and may he work in us what is pleasing to him, through Jesus Christ, to whom be glory for ever and ever. Amen.

Cross

1 Corinthians 1:18—The message of the cross is foolishness to those who are perishing, but to us who are being saved it is the power of God.

Galatians 6:14—May I never boast except in the cross of our Lord Jesus Christ, through which the world has been crucified to me, and I to the world.

Galatians 2:20—I have been crucified with Christ and I no longer live, but Christ lives in me. The life I now live in the body, I live by faith in the Son of God, who loved me and gave himself for me.

Romans 5:8-9—God demonstrates his own love for us in this: While we were still sinners, Christ died for us. Since we have now been justified by his blood, how much more shall we be saved from God's wrath through him!

Discernment

Hebrews 5:14—Solid food is for the mature, who by constant use have trained themselves to distinguish good from evil.

Proverbs 3:5-7—Trust in the Lord with all your heart and lean not on your own understanding; in all your ways submit to him, and he will make your paths straight. Do not be wise in your own eyes; fear the Lord and shun evil.

Psalm 1:1-3—Blessed is the one who does not walk in step with the wicked or stand in the way that sinners take or sit in the company of mockers, but whose delight is in the law of the Lord, and who meditates on his law day and night. That person is like a tree planted by streams of water, which yields its fruit in season and whose leaf does not wither—whatever they do prospers.

Psalm 34:11-14—Come, my children, listen to me; I will teach you the fear of the Lord. Whoever of you loves life and desires to see many good days, keep your tongue from evil and your lips from speaking lies. Turn from evil and do good; seek peace and pursue it.

Proverbs 2:10-13—Wisdom will enter your heart, and knowledge will be pleasant to your soul. Discretion will protect you, and understanding will guard you. Wisdom will save you from the ways of wicked men, from men whose words are perverse, who leave the straight paths to walk in dark ways.

Eternal Life

John 10:10—The thief comes only to steal and kill and destroy; I have come that they may have life, and have it to the full.

John 17:3—Now this is eternal life: that they know you, the only true God, and Jesus Christ, whom you have sent.

Romans 10:9-10—If you declare with your mouth, "Jesus is Lord," and believe in your heart that God raised him from the dead, you will be saved. For it is with your heart that you believe and are justified, and it is with your mouth that you profess your faith and are saved.

1 John 5:11-12—This is the testimony: God has given us eternal life, and this life is in his Son. Whoever has the Son has life; whoever does not have the Son of God does not have life.

Fear of the Lord

*Proverbs 1:7—The fear of the Lord is the beginning of knowledge, but fools despise wisdom and instruction.

Philippians 2:12-13—My dear friends, as you have always obeyed—not only in my presence, but now much more in my absence—continue to work out your salvation with fear and trembling, for it is God who works in you to will and to act in order to fulfill his good purpose.

Psalm 25:12-14—Who, then, are those who fear the Lord? He will instruct them in the ways they should choose. The Lord confides in those who fear him; he makes his covenant known to them.

Psalm 66:16-20—Come and hear, all you who fear God; let me tell you what he has done for me. I cried out to him with my mouth; his praise was on my tongue. If I had cherished sin in my heart, the Lord would not have listened; but God has surely listened and has heard my prayer. Praise be to God, who has not rejected my prayer or withheld his love from me!

Forgiveness

*1 John 1:9—If we confess our sins, he is faithful and just and will forgive us our sins and purify us from all unrighteousness.

Ephesians 4:31-32—Get rid of all bitterness, rage and anger, brawling and slander, along with every form of malice. Be kind and compassionate to one another, forgiving each other, just as in Christ God forgave you.

Psalm 25:16-18—Turn to me and be gracious to me, for I am lonely and afflicted. Relieve the troubles of my heart and free me from my anguish. Look on my affliction and my distress and take away all my sins.

Psalm 38:18-22—I confess my iniquity; I am troubled by my sin. Many have become my enemies without cause; those who repay my good with evil lodge accusations against me, though I seek only to do what is good. Lord, do not forsake me; do not be far from me, my God. Come quickly to help me, my Lord and my Savior.

Glory of God

*1 Corinthians 10:31—Whether you eat or drink or whatever you do, do it all for the glory of God.

2 Corinthians 3:18—We all, who with unveiled faces contemplate the Lord's glory, are being transformed into his image with ever-increasing glory, which comes from the Lord, who is the Spirit.

1 Chronicles 29:10-13—David praised the Lord in the presence of the whole assembly, saying, "Praise be to you, Lord, the God of our father Israel, from everlasting to everlasting. Yours, O Lord, is the greatness and the power and the glory and the majesty and the splendor, for everything in heaven and earth is yours. Yours, O Lord, is the kingdom; you are exalted as head over all. Wealth and honor come from you; you are the ruler of all things. In your hands are strength and power to exalt and give strength to all. Now, our God, we give you thanks, and praise your glorious name."

Psalm 19:1—The heavens declare the glory of God; the skies proclaim the work of his hands.

Ezekiel 43:2—I saw the glory of the God of Israel coming from the east. His voice was like the roar of rushing waters, and the land was radiant with his glory.

God

*Psalm 90:2—Before the mountains were born or you brought forth the whole world, from everlasting to everlasting you are God.

Romans 11:33—Oh, the depth of the riches of the wisdom and knowledge of God! How unsearchable his judgments, and his paths beyond tracing out!

Isaiah 40:25-26,28-29—"To whom will you compare me? Or who is my equal?" says the Holy One. Lift your eyes and look to the heavens: Who created all these? He who brings out the starry host one by one, and calls forth each of them by name. Because of his great power and mighty strength, not one of them is missing...Do you not know? Have you not heard? The LORD is the everlasting God, the Creator of the ends of the earth. He will not grow tired or weary, and his understanding no one can fathom. He gives strength to the weary and increases the power of the weak.

Isaiah 57:15—This is what the high and exalted One says—he who lives forever, whose name is holy: "I live in a high and holy place, but also with the one who is contrite and lowly in spirit, to revive the spirit of the lowly and to revive the heart of the contrite."

Daniel 4:35—All the peoples of the earth are regarded as nothing. He does as he pleases with the powers of heaven and the peoples of the earth. No one can hold back his hand or say to him: "What have you done?"

Hebrews 1:2-3—In these last days he has spoken to us by his Son, whom he appointed heir of all things, and through whom also he made the universe. The Son is the radiance of God's glory and the exact representation of his being, sustaining all things by his powerful word. After he had provided purification for sins, he sat down at the right hand of the Majesty in heaven.

Grace

Ephesians 2:8-9—It is by grace you have been saved, through faith— and this is not from yourselves, it is the gift of God—not by works, so that no one can boast.

2 Corinthians 12:9—He said to me, "My grace is sufficient for you, for my power is made perfect in weakness." Therefore I will boast all the more gladly about my weaknesses, so that Christ's power may rest on me.

Titus 3:5-7—He saved us, not because of righteous things we had done, but because of his mercy. He saved us through the washing of rebirth and renewal by the Holy Spirit, whom he poured out on us generously through Jesus Christ our Savior, so that, having been justified by his grace, we might become heirs having the hope of eternal life.

Grief

1 Thessalonians 4:13-14—Brothers and sisters, we do not want you to be uninformed about those who sleep in death, so that you do not grieve like the rest of mankind, who have no hope. For we believe that Jesus died and rose again and so we believe that God will bring with Jesus those who have fallen asleep in him.

Job 23:10—He knows the way that I take; when he has tested me, I will come forth as gold.

Romans 8:26-28—In the same way, the Spirit helps us in our weakness. We do not know what we ought to pray for, but the Spirit himself intercedes for us through wordless groans. And he who searches our hearts knows the mind of the Spirit, because the Spirit intercedes for God's people in accordance with the will of God. And we know that in all things God works for the good of those who love him, who have been called according to his purpose.

Heaven

Revelation 21:1-4—I saw "a new heaven and a new earth," for the first heaven and the first earth had passed away, and there was no longer any sea. I saw the Holy City, the new Jerusalem, coming down out of heaven from God, prepared as a bride beautifully dressed for her husband. And I heard a loud voice from the throne saying, "Look! God's dwelling place is now among the people, and he will dwell with them. They will be his people, and God himself will be with them and be their God. He will wipe every tear from their eyes. There will be no more death or mourning or crying or pain, for the old order of things has passed away."

Revelation 21:21-27—The twelve gates were twelve pearls, each gate made of a single pearl. The great street of the city was of gold, as pure as transparent glass. I did not see a temple in the city, because the Lord God Almighty and the Lamb are its temple. The city does not need the sun or the moon to shine on it, for the glory of God gives it light, and the Lamb is its lamp. The nations will walk by its light, and the kings of the earth will bring their splendor into it. On no day will its gates ever be shut, for there will be no night there. The glory and honor of the nations will be brought into it. Nothing impure will ever enter it, nor will anyone who does what is shameful or deceitful, but only those whose names are written in the Lamb's book of life.

Philippians 3:20-21—Our citizenship is in heaven. And we eagerly await a Savior from there, the Lord Jesus Christ, who, by the power that enables him to bring everything under his control, will transform our lowly bodies so that they will be like his glorious body.

Hell

Luke 12:5—I will show you whom you should fear: Fear him who, after your body has been killed, has authority to throw you into hell. Yes, I tell you, fear him.

Revelation 20:15—Anyone whose name was not found written in the book of life was thrown into the lake of fire.

Revelation 20:11-14—I saw a great white throne and him who was seated on it. The earth and the heavens fled from his presence, and there was no place for them. And I saw the dead, great and small, standing before the throne, and books were opened. Another book was opened, which is the book of life. The dead were judged according to what they had done as recorded in the books. The sea gave up the dead that were in it, and death and Hades gave up the dead that were in them, and each person was judged according to what they had done. Then death and Hades were thrown into the lake of fire. The lake of fire is the second death.

Holy Spirit

*John 7:37-39—On the last and greatest day of the festival, Jesus stood and said in a loud voice, "Let anyone who is thirsty come to me and drink. Whoever believes in me, as the Scripture has said, rivers of living water will flow from within them." By this he meant the Spirit, whom those who believed in him were later to receive. Up to that time the Spirit had not been given, since Jesus had not yet been glorified.

John 16:13—When he, the Spirit of truth, comes, he will guide you into all the truth. He will not speak on his own; he will speak only what he hears, and he will tell you what is yet to come.

Galatians 5:22-23—The fruit of the Spirit is love, joy, peace, patience, forbearance, goodness, faithfulness, gentleness and self-control. Against such things there is no law.

John 14:25-26—All this I have spoken while still with you. But the Advocate, the Holy Spirit, whom the Father will send in my name, will teach you all things and will remind you of everything I have said to you.

Romans 8:11—If the Spirit of him who raised Jesus from the dead is living in you, he who raised Christ from the dead will also give life to your mortal bodies because of his Spirit who lives in you.

Hebrews 9:14—How much more, then, will the blood of Christ, who through the eternal Spirit offered himself unblemished to God, cleanse our consciences from acts that lead to death, so that we may serve the living God!

Hope

*Romans 15:13—May the God of hope fill you with all joy and peace as you trust in him, so that you may overflow with hope by the power of the Holy Spirit.

Romans 8:28—We know that in all things God works for the good of those who love him, who have been called according to his purpose.

Psalm 39:7-8—But now, Lord, what do I look for? My hope is in you. Save me from all my transgressions; do not make me the scorn of fools.

Psalm 71:14-16—As for me, I will always have hope; I will praise you more and more. My mouth will tell of your righteous deeds, of your saving acts all day long—though I know not how to relate them all. I will come and proclaim your mighty acts, Sovereign LORD; I will proclaim your righteous deeds, yours alone.

Jesus

*John 1:1-4,14—In the beginning was the Word, and the Word was with God, and the Word was God. He was with God in the beginning. Through him all things were made; without him nothing was made that has been made. In him was life, and that life was the light of all mankind…The Word became flesh and made his dwelling among us.

We have seen his glory, the glory of the one and only Son, who came from the Father, full of grace and truth.

Luke 1:31,35—You will conceive and give birth to a son, and you are to call him Jesus…The angel answered, "The Holy Spirit will come on you, and the power of the Most High will overshadow you. So the holy one to be born will be called the Son of God."

John: 14:6—I am the way and the truth and the life. No one comes to the Father except through me.

John 10:11—I am the good shepherd. The good shepherd lays down his life for the sheep.

Hebrews 13:20-21—May the God of peace, who through the blood of the eternal covenant brought back from the dead our Lord Jesus, that great Shepherd of the sheep, equip you with everything good for doing his will, and may he work in us what is pleasing to him, through Jesus Christ, to whom be glory for ever and ever.

Hebrews 1:2-3—In these last days he has spoken to us by his Son, whom he appointed heir of all things, and through whom also he made the universe. The Son is the radiance of God's glory and the exact representation of his being, sustaining all things by his powerful word. After he had provided purification for sins, he sat down at the right hand of the Majesty in heaven.

Justification

*Romans 5:1-2—Since we have been justified through faith, we have peace with God through our Lord Jesus Christ, through whom we have gained access by faith into this grace in which we now stand. And we boast in the hope of the glory of God.

Romans 8:33-34—Who will bring any charge against those whom God has chosen? It is God who justifies. Who is the one who condemns? No one. Christ Jesus who died—more than that, who was raised to life—is at the right hand of God and is also interceding for us.

1 Corinthians 6:11—That is what some of you were. But you were washed, you were sanctified, you were justified in the name of the Lord Jesus Christ and by the Spirit of our God.

Loss

Job 1:21—Naked I came from my mother's womb, and naked I will depart. The LORD gave and the LORD has taken away; may the name of the LORD be praised.

Job 13:15—Though he slay me, yet will I hope in him; I will surely defend my ways to his face.

Romans 8:35-39—Who shall separate us from the love of Christ? Shall trouble or hardship or persecution or famine or nakedness or danger or sword? As it is written: "For your sake we face death all day long; we are considered as sheep to be slaughtered." No, in all these things we are more than conquerors through him who loved us. For I am convinced that neither death nor life, neither angels nor demons, neither the present nor the future, nor any powers, neither height nor depth, nor anything else in all creation, will be able to separate us from the love of God that is in Christ Jesus our Lord.

Love

1 Corinthians 13:1-3—If I speak in the tongues of men or of angels, but do not have love, I am only a resounding gong or a clanging cymbal. If I have the gift of prophecy and can fathom all mysteries and all knowledge, and if I have a faith that can move mountains, but do not have love, I am nothing. If I give all I possess to the poor and give over my body to hardship that I may boast, but do not have love, I gain nothing.

John 3:16—For God so loved the world that he gave his one and only Son, that whoever believes in him shall not perish but have eternal life.

Ephesians 2:4-5—Because of his great love for us, God, who is rich in mercy, made us alive with Christ even when we were dead in transgressions—it is by grace you have been saved.

Colossians 3:12-14—As God's chosen people, holy and dearly loved; clothe yourselves with compassion, kindness, humility, gentleness and patience. Bear with each other and forgive one another if any of you has a grievance against someone. Forgive as the Lord forgave you. And over all these virtues put on love, which binds them all together in perfect unity.

1 John 4:7-10—Dear friends, let us love one another, for love comes from God. Everyone who loves has been born of God and knows God. Whoever does not love does not know God, because God is love. This is how God showed his love among us: He sent his one and only Son into the world that we might live through him. This is love: not that we loved God, but that he loved us and sent his Son as an atoning sacrifice for our sins.

Peace

*John 14:27—Peace I leave with you; my peace I give you. I do not give to you as the world gives. Do not let your hearts be troubled and do not be afraid.

Philippians 4:7—The peace of God, which transcends all understanding, will guard your hearts and your minds in Christ Jesus.

Isaiah 26:3-4—You will keep in perfect peace those whose minds are steadfast, because they trust in you. Trust in the LORD forever, for the LORD, the LORD himself, is the Rock eternal.

Colossians 3:15—Let the peace of Christ rule in your hearts, since as members of one body you were called to peace. And be thankful.

Prayer

*Mark 1:35—Very early in the morning, while it was still dark, Jesus got up, left the house and went off to a solitary place, where he prayed.

Ephesians 6:18—Pray in the Spirit on all occasions with all kinds of prayers and requests. With this in mind, be alert and always keep on praying for all the Lord's people.

Psalm 119:147—I rise before dawn and cry for help; I have put my hope in your word.

Matthew 6:9-15—This, then, is how you should pray: "Our Father in heaven, hallowed be your name, your kingdom come, your will be done, on earth as it is in heaven. Give us today our daily bread. And forgive us our debts, as we also have forgiven our debtors. And lead us not into temptation, but deliver us from the evil one." For if you forgive other people when they sin against you, your heavenly Father will also forgive you. But if you do not forgive others their sins, your Father will not forgive your sins.

James 5:16—Confess your sins to each other and pray for each other so that you may be healed. The prayer of a righteous person is powerful and effective.

1 John 5:14-15—This is the confidence we have in approaching God: that if we ask anything according to his will, he hears us. And if we know that he hears us—whatever we ask—we know that we have what we asked of him.

Purity

*Matthew 5:8—Blessed are the pure in heart, for they will see God.

Romans 13:14—Rather, clothe yourselves with the Lord Jesus Christ, and do not think about how to gratify the desires of the flesh.

Psalm 19:12-14—Who can discern their own errors? Forgive my hidden faults. Keep your servant also from willful sins; may they not rule over me. Then I will be blameless, innocent of great transgression. May these words of my mouth and this meditation of my heart be pleasing in your sight, Lord, my Rock and my Redeemer.

Galatians 2:20—I have been crucified with Christ and I no longer live, but Christ lives in me. The life I live in the body, I live by faith in the Son of God, who loved me and gave himself for me.

1 Thessalonians 5:23-24—May God himself, the God of peace, sanctify you through and through. May your whole spirit, soul and body be kept blameless at the coming of our Lord Jesus Christ. The one who calls you is faithful, and he will do it.

1 Timothy 4:12—Don't let anyone look down on you because you are young, but set an example for the believers in speech, in conduct, in love, in faith and in purity.

2 Timothy 2:22—Flee the evil desires of youth and pursue righteousness, faith, love and peace, along with those who call on the Lord out of a pure heart.

Redemption

*1 Peter 1:18-19—You know that it was not with perishable things such as silver or gold that you were redeemed from the empty way of life handed down to you from your ancestors, but with the precious blood of Christ, a lamb without blemish or defect.

Ephesians 1:7-8—In him we have redemption through his blood, the forgiveness of sins, in accordance with the riches of God's grace that he lavished on us.

Hebrews 9:12—He did not enter by means of the blood of goats and calves; but he entered the Most Holy Place once for all by his own blood, having obtained eternal redemption.

Renewing the Mind

*Romans 12:1-2—I urge you, brothers and sisters, in view of God's mercy, to offer your bodies as a living sacrifice, holy and pleasing to God—this is your true and proper worship. Do not conform to the pattern of this

world, but be transformed by the renewing of your mind. Then you will be able to test and approve what God's will is—his good, pleasing and perfect will.

2 Corinthians 10:5—We demolish arguments and every pretension that sets itself up against the knowledge of God, and we take captive every thought to make it obedient to Christ.

Philippians 4:8—Finally, brothers and sisters, whatever is true, whatever is noble, whatever is right, whatever is pure, whatever is lovely, whatever is admirable—if anything is excellent or praiseworthy—think about such things.

Psalm 19:12-14—Who can discern their own errors? Forgive my hidden faults. Keep your servant also from willful sins; may they not rule over me. Then I will be blameless, innocent of great transgression. May these words of my mouth and this meditation of my heart be pleasing in your sight, Lord, my Rock and my Redeemer.

Rewards

*1 Corinthians 3:13-15—Their work will be shown for what it is, because the Day will bring it to light. It will be revealed with fire, and the fire will test the quality of each person's work. If what has been built survives, the builder will receive a reward. If it is burned up, the builder will suffer loss but yet will be saved—even though only as one escaping through the flames.

2 Corinthians 5:10—We must all appear before the judgment seat of Christ, so that each of us may receive what is due us for the things done while in the body, whether good or bad.

Matthew 25:21—His master replied, "Well done, good and faithful servant! You have been faithful with a few things; I will put you in charge of many things. Come and share your master's happiness!"

2 Timothy 4:7-8—I have fought the good fight, I have finished the race,

I have kept the faith. Now there is in store for me the crown of righteousness, which the Lord, the righteous Judge, will award to me on that day—and not only to me, but also to all who have longed for his appearing.

Psalm 62:11-12—One thing God has spoken, two things have I heard: "Power belongs to you, God, and with you, Lord, is unfailing love"; and, "You reward everyone according to what they have done."

Satan

*1 Peter 5:8-9—Be alert and of sober mind. Your enemy the devil prowls around like a roaring lion looking for someone to devour. Resist him, standing firm in the faith, because you know that the family of believers throughout the world is undergoing the same kind of sufferings.

James 4:7-8—Submit yourselves, then, to God. Resist the devil, and he will flee from you. Come near to God and he will come near to you. Wash your hands, you sinners, and purify your hearts, you double-minded.

Revelation 20:10—The devil, who deceived them, was thrown into the lake of burning sulfur, where the beast and the false prophet had been thrown. They will be tormented day and night for ever and ever.

Second Coming

*Titus 2:11-14—The grace of God has appeared that offers salvation to all people. It teaches us to say "No" to ungodliness and worldly passions, and to live self-controlled, upright and godly lives in this present age, while we wait for the blessed hope—the appearing of the glory of our great God and Savior, Jesus Christ, who gave himself for us to redeem us from all wickedness and to purify for himself a people that are his very own, eager to do what is good.

1 John 3:2-3—Dear friends, now we are children of God, and what we will be has not yet been made known. But we know that when Christ appears, we shall be like him, for we shall see him as he is. All who have this hope in him purify themselves, just as he is pure.

1 Corinthians 15:51-52—Listen, I tell you a mystery: We will not all sleep, but we will all be changed—in a flash, in the twinkling of an eye, at the last trumpet. For the trumpet will sound, the dead will be raised imperishable, and we will be changed.

Sensuality

Matthew 5:27-30—You have heard that it was said, "Do not commit adultery." But I tell you that anyone who looks at a woman lustfully has already committed adultery with her in his heart. If your right eye causes you to stumble, gouge it out and throw it away. It is better for you to lose one part of your body than for your whole body to be thrown into hell. And if your right hand causes you to stumble, cut it off and throw it away. It is better for you to lose one part of your body than for your whole body to go into hell.

Psalm 119:9—How can a young person stay on the path of purity? By living according to your word.

1 Corinthians 6:18-20—Flee from sexual immorality. All other sins a person commits are outside the body, but whoever sins sexually, sins against their own body. Do you not know that your bodies are temples of the Holy Spirit, who is in you, whom you have received from God? You are not your own; you were bought at a price. Therefore honor God with your bodies.

Sin

Romans 3:23—All have sinned and fall short of the glory of God.

Psalm 38:1-4—Lord, do not rebuke me in your anger or discipline me in your wrath. Your arrows have pierced me, and your hand has come down on me. Because of your wrath there is no health in my body; there is no soundness in my bones because of my sin. My guilt has overwhelmed me like a burden too heavy to bear.

John 8:34-36—Very truly I tell you, everyone who sins is a slave to sin. Now a slave has no permanent place in the family, but a son belongs to it forever. So if the Son sets you free, you will be free indeed.

Romans 6:12-13—Do not let sin reign in your mortal body so that you obey its evil desires. Do not offer any part of yourself to sin as an instrument of wickedness, but rather offer yourselves to God as those who have been brought from death to life; and offer every part of yourself to him as an instrument of righteousness.

Temptation

*1 Corinthians 10:13—No temptation has overtaken you except what is common to mankind. And God is faithful; he will not let you be tempted beyond what you can bear. But when you are tempted, he will also provide a way out so that you can endure.

Psalm 71:1-2—In you, LORD, I have taken refuge; let me never be put to shame. In your righteousness, rescue me and deliver me; turn your ear to me and save me.

1 Thessalonians 4:3-4—It is God's will that you should be sanctified: that you should avoid sexual immorality; that each of you should learn to control your own body in a way that is holy and honorable.

James 1:13-15—When tempted, no one should say, "God is tempting me." For God cannot be tempted by evil, nor does he tempt anyone; but each one is tempted when they are dragged away by their own evil desire and enticed. Then, after desire has conceived, it gives birth to sin; and sin, when it is full-grown, gives birth to death.

Thanksgiving

*1 Thessalonians 5:16-18—Rejoice always, pray continually, give thanks in all circumstances; for this is God's will for you in Christ Jesus.

Psalm 100:4-5—Enter his gates with thanksgiving and his courts with praise; give thanks to him and praise his name. For the LORD is good and his love endures forever; his faithfulness continues through all generations.

Ephesians 5:19-20—Sing and make music from your heart to the Lord, always giving thanks to God the Father for everything, in the name of our Lord Jesus Christ.

Colossians 1:3-4—We always thank God, the Father of our Lord Jesus Christ, when we pray for you, because we have heard of your faith in Christ Jesus and of the love you have for all God's people.

James 1:2-4—Consider it pure joy, my brothers and sisters, whenever you face trials of many kinds, because you know that the testing of your faith produces perseverance. Let perseverance finish its work so that you may be mature and complete, not lacking anything.

Will of God

*1 Thessalonians 4:3-4; 5:17-18—It is God's will that you should be sanctified: that you should avoid sexual immorality; that each of you should learn to control your own body in a way that is holy and honorable... Pray continually, give thanks in all circumstances; for this is God's will for you in Christ Jesus.

Philippians 3:12-14—Not that I have already obtained all this, or have already arrived at my goal, but I press on to take hold of that for which Christ Jesus took hold of me. Brothers and sisters, I do not consider myself yet to have taken hold of it. But one thing I do: Forgetting what is behind and straining toward what is ahead, I press on toward the goal to win the prize for which God has called me heavenward in Christ Jesus.

Colossians 2:6-7—Just as you received Christ Jesus as Lord, continue to live your lives in him, rooted and built up in him, strengthened in the faith as you were taught, and overflowing with thankfulness.

Wisdom

James 1:5-6—If any of you lacks wisdom, you should ask God, who gives generously to all without finding fault, and it will be given to you. But when you ask, you must believe and not doubt, because the one who doubts is like a wave of the sea, blown and tossed by the wind.

Psalm 119:34-37—Give me understanding, so that I may keep your law and obey it with all my heart. Direct me in the path of your commands, for there I find delight. Turn my heart toward your statutes and not toward selfish gain. Turn my eyes away from worthless things; preserve my life according to your word.

Proverbs 2:2-7—Turning your ear to wisdom and applying your heart to understanding—indeed, if you call out for insight and cry aloud for understanding, and if you look for it as for silver and search for it as for hidden treasure, then you will understand the fear of the LORD and find the knowledge of God. For the LORD gives wisdom; from his mouth come knowledge and understanding. He holds success in store for the upright, he is a shield to those whose walk is blameless.

2 Peter 1:3-4—His divine power has given us everything we need for a godly life through our knowledge of him who called us by his own glory and goodness. Through these he has given us his very great and precious promises, so that through them you may participate in the divine nature, having escaped the corruption in the world caused by evil desires.

Witnessing

Matthew 5:14-16—You are the light of the world. A town built on a hill cannot be hidden. Neither do people light a lamp and put it under a bowl. Instead they put it on its stand, and it gives light to everyone in the house. In the same way, let your light shine before others, that they may see your good deeds and glorify your Father in heaven.

1 Peter 3:15—In your hearts revere Christ as Lord. Always be prepared to give an answer to everyone who asks you to give the reason for the hope that you have. But do this with gentleness and respect.

Matthew 28:19-20—Go and make disciples of all nations, baptizing them in the name of the Father and of the Son and of the Holy Spirit, and teaching them to obey everything I have commanded you. And surely I am with you always, to the very end of the age.

2 Timothy 4:2—Preach the word; be prepared in season and out of season; correct, rebuke and encourage—with great patience and careful instruction.

Word of God

*Hebrews 4:12—The word of God is alive and active. Sharper than any double-edged sword, it penetrates even to dividing soul and spirit, joints and marrow; it judges the thoughts and attitudes of the heart.

2 Timothy 3:14-17—As for you, continue in what you have learned and have become convinced of, because you know those from whom you learned it, and how from infancy you have known the Holy Scriptures, which are able to make you wise for salvation through faith in Christ Jesus. All Scripture is God-breathed and is useful for teaching, rebuking, correcting and training in righteousness, so that the servant of God may be thoroughly equipped for every good work.

Psalm 19:7-11—The law of the LORD is perfect, refreshing the soul. The statutes of the LORD are trustworthy, making wise the simple. The precepts of the LORD are right, giving joy to the heart. The commands of the LORD are radiant, giving light to the eyes. The fear of the LORD is pure, enduring forever. The decrees of the LORD are firm, and all of them are righteous. They are more precious than gold, than much pure gold; they are sweeter than honey, than honey from the honeycomb. By them is your servant warned; in keeping them there is great reward.

Psalm 119:105—Your word is a lamp for my feet, a light on my path.

NOTES

1. Stephen L. Carter, *Integrity* (New York: Basic Books, 1996).

2. Warren Wiersbe, *The Wycliffe Handbook of Preaching & Preachers* (Chicago: Moody, 1984), p. 194.

3. "Calvary Covers It All," by Mrs. Walter G. Taylor (1934).

4. William P. Farley, *Gospel-Powered Parenting* (Phillipsburg, NJ: P&R Publishing, 2009), p. 63.

5. "The Fear of the Lord" quoted in Carol W. Cornish, *The Undistracted Widow* (Wheaton, IL: Crossway, 2010), p. 104.

6. This paragraph is derived from the doctrinal statement of The Moody Church (Chicago).

7. John Newton, "Amazing Grace," published 1779.

8. Jan Glidewell, as cited at www.thinkexist.com.

9. John Piper, "Discerning Idolatry in Desire," at http://desiringgod.org/ResourceLibrary/Taste AndSee/By Date2009/3991.

10. M.R. DeHaan, *Revelation* (Grand Rapids: Zondervan, 1946), p. 281.

11. *Merriam-Webster's Collegiate Dictionary*, 11th ed. (Springfield, MA: Merriam-Webster, 2003), s.v. "synergism."

12. Walter Baxendale, *Dictionary of Anecdote, Incident, Illustrative Fact Selected and Arranged for the Pulpit and the Platform* (London: Dickinson, 1903), p. 428.

13. Everett F. Harrison, *Baker's Dictionary of Theology* (Grand Rapids: Baker, 1973), p. 439.

14. Fanny J. Crosby, "Redeemed," written circa 1882.

15. From a sermon by Benjamin Needler, "How May Beloved Lusts Be Discovered and Mortified?" as cited by Classic Protestant Texts at http://solomon.tcpt.alexanderstreet.com/cgi-bin/asp/philo/cpt/getobject.pl?c.1002:2:3.cpt.

16. William P. Farley, *Gospel-Powered Parenting* (Phillipsburg, NJ: P&R Publishing, 2009), p. 95.

17. Timothy Lane and Paul David Tripp, *How People Change* (Greensboro, NC: New Growth Press, 2006), p. 5.

18. Lewis B. Smedes, *Shame and Grace* (San Francisco: HarperSanFrancisco, 1993), p. 116.

19. Lisa Beamer with Ken Abraham, *Let's Roll!* (Wheaton, IL: Tyndale, 2003), p. 281.

20. Marvin R. Vincent, *Word Studies in the New Testament,* vol. IV (Peabody, MA: Hendrickson, n.d.), p. 428.

21. Kenneth S. Wuest, *Hebrews in the Greek New Testament* (Grand Rapids: Eerdmans, 1956), p. 89.